EXPERT PUTTING

The science behind the stroke

Chris Riddoch

Expert Putting
http://www.TheGolfSwingZone.com

Image credits
Bigstock: Figure 8, handball goalkeeper
Shutterstock: cover; silhouette figures for Parts 1, 2, 3, & 4
Thinkstock: illustrations for chapter headings 1, 2, 3, 5, 7, & 9
Istock: illustrations for chapter headings 4, 6, 8, & 10

Bernard Darwin's quotes were taken from 'Tee Shots and Others', originally published by Kegan Paul, Trench, Trubner & Co. Ltd. London; 1911. No current copyright holder could be located.

For Hannah and Sarah

Contents

List of figures

Acknowledgements

This book covers many branches of science relevant to putting, and could not have been written without input from other scientists. I am particularly grateful for the expertise and assistance provided by the following colleagues:

Brian Holmes, Professor of Physics, San Jose State University;
Robert Grober, Professor of Physics, Yale University;
Anders Ericsson, Professor of Psychology, Florida State University;
Joan Vickers, Professor of Kinesiology, University of Calgary;
Ken Ravizza, Professor of Applied Sports Psychology, California State University, Fullerton.

I am also indebted to Philip Lindner, a golfing colleague who advised on content, style, and readability. Finally, I would like to thank the many scientists around the world, who carried out the high-quality research that forms the basis of this book.

Chris Riddoch is a professor of sports science, who has published more than 200 scientific articles on sport and exercise. A scratch golfer in his teens, he represented his college (Borough Road), his county (Cheshire), and had two trials for England (not selected, alas). He is married to Maya, and they live in Stockholm.

Putting is pre-eminently the department of the game with which each man must wrestle by himself in silence and sorrow.

—Bernard Darwin, 1911

1

Introduction

WE ALL DO IT, far too many times for it to be bad luck—we miss a putt, and we've no idea why. We judged speed and line, concentrated hard, swung like a pendulum, but missed. We're left wondering how we can try so hard, to do something so apparently simple, yet fail. The aim of this book is to solve the mystery, and explain how any of us can become an expert putter.

The first book in the series – 'The Golf Swing: it's easier than you think' – covered the science behind the full golf swing. It explained how to hit more balls into the fairway, and onto the green. This second book completes our golfing armoury: it explains the science of the next task—getting the ball into the hole.

And we're lucky, because not only do we understand the science of expert putting, we can apply it to our putting strokes through simple practices. In other words, there's nothing to stop any of us improving our putting. There's no secret, no complicated movements, and no new theories. Just the simple science of how putting 'works'.

Our main hurdle is to overcome the common belief that putting is a purely mechanical skill. Yes, mechanics are involved, but we move the putterhead only a matter of feet, or inches—it's a desperately simple movement. But the simplicity is the problem. It tempts us to believe that if we could just find the perfect combination of grip, stance, swing, and putter, we'd rid ourselves of our putting woes. But most of us still have woes, so there's clearly something missing.

Unfortunately, by focusing on mechanics, we ignore the real core of expert putting—*motor control*. Motor control simply means using the brain to control the body. The key point is that an expert putting stroke isn't just a mechanical movement, it's a complex skill that *combines* mechanics with the mental processes that control them.

We'll see in this book that the putting skill consists of four key elements:

- **Vision** - gathering information;
- **Imagery** – 'seeing' the putt;
- **Attention** – swing thoughts;
- **Mechanical control** – putterhead movement.

If we want to become expert putters, we need to develop all four links in this biological chain. This book describes how to do just that, by explaining the science behind the complete putting skill. To start things off, we'll clarify what *skill* is, and how we can get some.

Putting skill

In January 2011, Adrian Lewis won the Professional Darts Corporation World Championship, at Alexandra Palace in London. During the tournament, Adrian achieved a world record, by scoring 60 'maximums'. A maximum is a score of 180 with three darts, and to achieve it, a player must throw all three darts from a distance of just under eight feet into the treble 20. The treble 20 is a small, rectangular section of the dartboard, measuring just 0.35 inches high by 1.3 inches wide—that's smaller than a triple-A battery, or a pen top. It's so small that the thrower has to locate the first two darts in such a way that there's enough room for the third dart to find its way in.

Putting is a similar precision aiming skill, but we don't achieve the same skill levels as darts players. We have some limitations, in that we need to hit the ball with a putter, and we stand in the worst possible position from which to take aim, but even when tournament professionals putt from eight feet at their 4.25-inch wide target – three times the width of the treble 20 – they mostly miss. The point is, we underperform in the putting skill, and there's huge scope for improvement.

As we've already said, putting is a motor control problem. To be more precise, it's a *motor skill* problem. A motor skill is a package of muscle contractions, planned, delivered, and controlled by our brains. The quality of every putt we hit depends on how effectively our brains plan and control our movements.[i]

Many top players use psychologists, motor skill experts, and vision coaches to develop their skills, but most of us don't have such resources, so we tend to flounder in a morass of tips, opinions, and

---

[i] To be even more precise, putting is a *perceptual* motor skill: perceptual = brain; motor = body.

good ideas. But if we can understand the four elements of the putting skill, there's no reason why any of us can't develop them, and achieve expert status. And this is where science comes in, because science has the answers.

Putting science

The good thing about science is that it works. When we want to know the truth about something, we get it from science. The bad thing about science is that it can be complicated—sometimes impenetrable. And the science of putting is particularly complicated, because it involves many disciplines, including maths, physics, geometry, psychology, biomechanics, and neuroscience. In this book, we'll use the good, and we'll avoid the bad. We'll get to the truth about putting, and we'll simplify everything.

And we're not short of information. Millions of pounds have been invested in research to discover the essential ingredients of expert putting, so we can call on a massive evidence base, generated by top scientists from some of the world's best research facilities. We can even take the sophisticated science behind the rehabilitation of stroke patients, and use it to improve our putting. We no longer need to rely on tips, opinions, or untested theories— we can use proven facts. Although this book runs to just over 100 pages, the underlying science exceeds 10,000 pages! Annex 4 contains a select bibliography of studies used to compile the book.

To aid readability, some simplifications and standardisations have been made in the text. First, when studying putting, researchers often compare extremes, such as professionals with amateurs, or low- and high-handicap players. In this book, we've adopted the terms 'experts' and 'non-experts' when describing this research.

Second, science works in metric units (centimetres and metres), but because golf tradition favours imperial units (inches and feet), these have been used throughout the text. Finally, all scientific jargon has either been removed, translated into simpler language, or explained in footnotes. Footnotes are numbered consecutively, within chapters.

So now, we can get started. The book follows the three phases of the putt:

- **Part 1:** *Weighing it up* – judging speed and line;
- **Part 2:** *Preparing the stroke* – creating a mental plan;
- **Part 3:** *The stroke* – mechanics and control.

We'll then conclude with a section on how we can make changes that will improve our putting:

- **Part 4:** *Making it happen* – practice and mental approach.

First, *weighing it up*.

\\/ \\/ \\/   \\/ \\/ \\/

Part 1

Weighing it up

The non-golfer always feels an utter contempt for the golfer ... for the length of time which he devotes to his intensely solemn preliminaries. The spectacle of an eminent player grovelling deep in thought over a putt of four feet is to him simply absurd.... The prolonged walkings up and down, ponderings, crouching, and consultations with caddies add greatly to the excitement ... a little of it is splendid fun.

—Bernard Darwin, 1911

2

Judging speed

MOST OF US BELIEVE that leaving any putt short of the hole is a cardinal sin: 'must give the hole a chance …'. Hence, most of us try to putt at a speed that will take the ball past the hole if it misses. But we know this increases the risk of lip outs and three putting, so where's the best stopping place for us to aim at? We can find the answer by applying some simple physics—the physics of *ball capture*.

Ball capture: when ball meets hole

We understand three putting, but we may not fully understand lip outs. To get a better handle on this, we need to investigate how the hole captures the ball, if the two make contact. There are various suggestions regarding the best aiming distance. Many coaches say "a foot past the hole". The best-known suggestion comes from Dave

Pelz, who suggests we aim 17 inches past, because at this speed, the heavily trafficked, damaged surface around the hole doesn't affect the ball's roll.[i] But aiming past the hole may not always be the best strategy, as we'll see.

Brian Holmes, Professor of Physics at San Jose State University, has some interesting thoughts (and calculations) on this topic. He has no problem with aiming a foot past the hole for short putts (say, up to five feet), but for longer putts he suggests that even one foot past is too far. As putt length increases beyond five feet, the stopping distance past the hole should reduce, and for any putt outside 20 feet, the stopping point should *be* the hole. He's calculated that for an average ability putter, aiming past the hole for all putts, irrespective of distance, costs three strokes per round.

To see how this happens, we'll consider two scenarios: a ball arriving dead centre, and a ball arriving off centre. First, the dead-centre arrival.

Dead-centre arrival

When a ball arrives at the front centre rim of the hole, will gravity pull it in, or will it stay on the rim? The answer is that the hole will capture the ball if the arrival speed is at least 1.5 feet per second. At this speed, the ball enters free fall into the hole. At lower arrival speeds, the ball tends to hover on the rim before – if we're lucky – toppling over the edge. This is a little too close for comfort, so we should accept 1.5 feet per second as our *minimum capture speed*.

At higher arrival speeds, the hole will continue to capture the ball cleanly, until we reach speeds where things start to go wrong. At higher speeds, the ball, instead of falling cleanly into the hole, can

_____

[i] From reference 8.

do one of three things: hit the opposite rim, bounce in the air, and drop back into the hole; hit the far rim, bounce in the air, and stop somewhere beyond the hole; fly straight over the hole as if it wasn't there. We're just concerned with achieving capture by any method, clean or unclean, so we need to know the maximum arrival speed that will result in a holed putt. There's no need to go into the detailed maths, we can go straight to the answer: the hole will capture the ball if the arrival speed is less than 5.3 feet per second.[ii] This is our *maximum capture speed*.

These minimum and maximum capture speeds apply to a level green, so strictly speaking, we should apply a small correction for uphill and downhill putts. For putts up a five-degree slope, the maximum capture speed increases to 5.6 feet per second. For downhill putts on the same slope, it decreases to 5.1 feet per second.[iii] In practical terms, our putting skills aren't up to dealing with such small differences, so we can take the maximum arrival speed for a holed putt to be not too far away from 5.3 feet per second.

Unfortunately, we can't relate to arrival speeds, because they're just numbers. To be of any use, we need to translate them into how hard to hit the putt, or how far past the hole to aim. We'll deal with this shortly, but we need to stick with arrival speeds for just a little longer, while we deal with the *off-centre arrival*.

Off-centre arrival

The ball can still fall into the hole even if it arrives off centre. It can fall in directly, bounce into the hole off the far rim, or roll around the rim and then fall in. On the other hand, it can roll around the rim and lip out, or fly clean over the hole as before, so we need to

---

[ii] Data for capture speeds taken from reference 4.
[iii] Data taken from reference 9.

know the maximum capture speeds for balls arriving different amounts off centre. Capture speeds will be lower than for a dead-centre arrival, but we need to know by how much.

We could easily calculate maximum capture speeds for any off-centre arrival point, but there are so many possible arrival points, we'd just end up with a large and complicated set of numbers. But there's a simpler way. We know that putts lip out when they're travelling too fast, so faster-travelling balls make the hole effectively *smaller*. And this is far more useful, because we understand the concept of bigger or smaller holes. So now, we can translate. We can work out an *effective hole diameter* for any arrival speed. Figure 1 shows a graph of effective hole diameters at all arrival speeds between the minimum and maximum capture speeds.

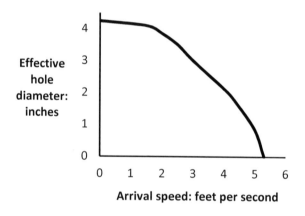

Figure 1. Effective hole diameter at different arrival speeds.[iv]

[iv] Figure adapted from reference 4.

Looking at Figure 1, we can see that the hole is only its full diameter of 4.25 inches for a ball arriving at the minimum capture speed of 1.5 feet per second. That is, a ball 'dying' into the hole. And at the other end of the graph, we can see that for any arrival speed greater than the maximum capture speed of 5.3 feet per second, the effective hole diameter is zero, because the ball will fly straight over the hole.

In between these extremes, we have what we're looking for: how much smaller we make the hole when we putt at higher speeds. For example, we can see that a ball arriving at a speed of 4.0 feet per second encounters a half-size hole—just 2.125 inches wide. We can also see that an arrival speed of 4.5 feet per second reduces the hole diameter to the diameter of the ball—1.68 inches. Not much room for error there ….

Always up, never in

We can now decide what distance to aim for, by considering a simple example. Consider the five-foot putt in Figure 2.

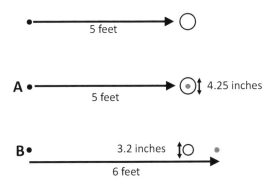

Figure 2. Effective hole diameter when aiming dead weight at the centre of the hole (A), and one foot past the hole (B).

For this putt, we don't want to aim dead length (A), because although we'll have the full 4.25-inches hole diameter to aim at, we'll leave half our putts short. Our solution is to aim one foot past, giving us a total putt distance of six feet (B). Again, we won't bother with the maths, but a six-foot putt gives us a hole diameter of 3.2 inches.[v]

The key point in this example is that aiming a five-foot putt one foot past the hole reduces our target size by almost *25 percent*. Are we happy with this? If not, we have only one option — don't aim so far past. It's all about how brave we feel. Are we confident we can hit a 3.2-inch wide hole from five feet?

An interesting approach to deciding how far past the hole to aim is to consider the ideal stopping point as two feet past, multiplied by the likelihood of holing the putt.[vi] If the likelihood of holing a putt is 50 percent (a putt of four to five feet), we should aim one foot (50 percent of two feet) past the hole. For putts where the likelihood of holing is 10 percent (a putt of 8-10 feet), we should aim just over two inches (10 percent of two feet) past. And at 20 feet, where we hole only around five percent of putts, we should aim *at* the hole (five percent of two feet is just over an inch).

This means that in practical terms, there's no perfect stopping distance past the hole, it's a function of putt length and confidence level. But one thing is clear: only on putts of less than 20 feet should we aim past the hole at all, and even then, we should aim a shorter distance past than most of us do at present. Clearly, by aiming closer to the hole we'll leave some well-directed putts short, but we'll be more than compensated by holing a greater proportion of

---

[v] Data kindly provided by Professor Brian Holmes.
[vi] Described in reference 3.

putts that make contact with the hole, and by having fewer three putts.

Attacking the hole

It's common to see even tournament professionals putting with speed from short distance, missing, and leaving long return putts. It's clear they decided to putt with excess speed in order to 'kill the break'—to make it a 'straight' putt. This isn't a good idea. First, the ball will always take some break, it will never be completely straight. Second, the excess speed makes the target smaller, as we've seen. Third, harder strokes have greater risk of error. Fourth, we may have the same problem with the return putt.

The safest approach to a short, breaking putt is to treat it just like any other putt—choose the perfect speed and line, and make a normal stroke. This ensures we have maximum target size, maximum chance of ball capture, minimum risk of stroke errors, and virtually no risk of three putting. The perfect speed and line is exactly what it says—the perfect speed and line.

From greater distances, hitting putts harder than necessary, to ensure the ball reaches the hole, has one small advantage, but all the disadvantages we've just covered. The advantage is that if we slightly under hit the putt, the ball might still fall into the hole. But will it? There are some serious concerns about how true this is, so we should investigate a little further.

Consider a 10-foot putt with one foot of break. We can programme a putting robot to putt on a speed–line combination that will hole the putt every time. But if we vary the speed by just three percent – either higher or lower – the robot misses. Three percent is a tiny margin of error that we can't achieve. Even tournament professionals can only control putting distance to around 10 percent of the putt length, so it's no surprise they miss most 10-foot putts. In reality, an under-hit putt with any amount of break rarely finds the hole, because the line we launched it on is wrong for the lower speed.

While we're on the topic of distance control, we might also consider our own skill in this department. Many of us struggle to control distance to within 20 percent of putt length, so if we aim all our putts one foot past, irrespective of distance, we'll be leaving many short anyway.[vii] In fact, to ensure we never leave a 20-foot putt short, we need to aim almost five feet past—so we'll be facing return putts of up to *10 feet*. Except for short putts, always aiming past the hole is a debatable strategy.

All of the above suggests that we'd be wise to adopt a new concept of 'attacking the hole'. Currently, we view attacking the hole as 'charging' the putt at high speed. We often do this, and the ball lips out, or we three putt. But we take comfort in the fact that at least we were being positive. Unfortunately, we weren't. Given what we know about ball capture, and how many return putts most of us miss, this strategy simply inflates our scores. The true meaning of attacking the hole is giving the hole the maximum chance of capturing the ball, so the best attacking putt will just 'die' over the lip. The problem here is that if we miss a crucial putt by leaving it a few inches short, we'll receive endless criticism from partner or caddie for committing the cardinal putting sin. But the critics don't know the maths.

[vii] Distance control must be measured during competition: different greens, random length putts, no previous putts to learn from, and only one attempt. It's worse than we think ....

Finally, should any of us still think that always aiming past the hole is a good idea, there's yet another way it can work against us. It happens when we think "I mustn't be short". Unfortunately, the human brain uses the same control system to monitor 'do' commands and 'don't' commands, and it sometimes mixes them up. When we think 'don't be short', our brains can activate the 'do' command—and leave it short.[viii] The human brain sometimes works in mysterious ways.

So now, we have a better grasp of judging speed. Next, we'll consider how to judge *line*. And for this, we need to move away from maths and physics, and into geometry.

[viii] We call this an *ironic process*.

PUTTING KEYS

1 The best aiming distance past the hole is shorter than we think.

1 The best aiming distance varies with putt length and confidence level.

1 For putts of 20 feet or more, our best strategy is to aim at the hole.

1 The best attacking putt arrives at the hole with minimum speed.

1 In putting, speed kills.

3

Judging line

S LOPES CAUSE THE BALL TO CURVE, which makes putting more difficult. In some aiming sports, such as lawn bowls, or ten-pin
bowling, players also have curving balls to deal with, but they don't
have slopes to negotiate, so the ball curves consistently. They
simply need to decide how much left or right to aim. But in putting,
we face an infinite variety of slopes and slope combinations, so aiming is harder. We'll consider two circumstances in which slopes affect aim: putts straight up and down the slope, and putts across the
slope.

Uphill and down dale

We might think that when putting straight uphill or downhill, the
slope only affects speed. Aiming isn't a problem, we just aim dead
centre. But uphill and downhill putts are subtly different, because

19

one is more difficult to hole. And it's the opposite of what we might expect—uphill putts are harder.

Consider a straight, uphill putt. If we start the ball slightly off line, the slope causes the ball to diverge further off line. The slope *magnifies* our original error. On the other hand, if we make the same error in the equivalent downhill putt, the slope causes the ball to converge back towards the hole. The slope *reduces* our error.[i] We can see these effects in Figure 3.

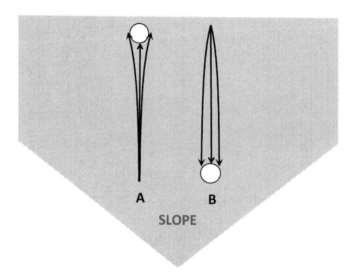

Figure 3. Effects of slope on putt trajectory for uphill (A), and down-hill (B) putts.[ii]

It's simple to understand. A straight uphill putt is only straight if we hit it directly at the centre of the hole. If we stray off line, we're putting slightly across the slope, so the putt takes the break and veers away from the hole. The reverse happens for downhill putts,

---

[i] From reference 9.

[ii] Adapted from reference 9.

where off-line putts break back towards the hole. In other words, downhill putts are *self-correcting*. Faster greens magnify the effect, so uphill putts become even harder to hole, and downhill putts even easier. This is because fast putts roll slowly, giving the slope more time to exert its effects. Again, this is the opposite of what many of us believe—while we think downhill putts are hard, we think fast downhill putts are all but impossible. But the probability of holing a 10-foot putt downhill is three times greater than holing it uphill—a huge difference. We should enjoy downhill putts.

But we don't. We dislike them, and it's easy to see why—we're afraid of speed. And it's good that we're afraid, because there's clearly a trade-off between having a greater chance of ball capture, and an increased risk of leaving the ball a long way past the hole if we miss. For example, consider a 10-foot uphill putt launched to leave the ball three feet past the hole (a little too far, but not a disaster). The equivalent putt downhill, delivered to achieve the same arrival speed (and hence an equal chance of capture) would leave the ball *13 feet* past the hole—an utter disaster.[iii]

In reality, downhill putts frighten us, not because they're more difficult to hole – quite the opposite – but because we want to avoid three putting. But if we have just one putt for the club championship—we need it to be straight, fast, and downhill.

Traversing slopes

When we putt a ball across a slope, it follows a predictable trajectory towards the hole. The science of trajectories is sophisticated, and we use it to assess many useful things: how much fuel a train

---

[iii] All data on slope effects taken from reference 9.

uses over hilly countryside; the best glide trajectory for an aeroplane after its engine fails; a skier's fastest line of descent down and across a slope.[iv] And we can use the same science to analyse the perfect putting trajectory.

We know that a range of speed–line combinations will take the ball to the hole. Harder putts take less break. But which combination is best? We'll again skip the maths, and jump straight to the answer: the ball has the greatest chance of capture when it arrives at the hole with the minimum capture speed, so we need to launch it at the *highest* angle. For any breaking putt, the slow high road to the hole is always best. Our next problem is judging how high the high road is. That is, exactly where should we aim?

I think it's a bit from the left …

Dave Pelz calculated that most of us read only 25–35 percent of a putt's break—a staggering underestimation.[v] This suggests that we should miss every breaking putt badly on the low side, but we don't. We do miss more putts on the low side, but not by the amount that our terrible reading errors suggest. We under-read the break, yet we somehow manage to putt on something closer to the correct line. We'll learn more about how this happens in Chapter 4, but now, we need to delve a little deeper into the science of reading the correct amount of break. And for this, we need to understand the work of Air Force Colonel Horace A. Templeton.

Horace Templeton engineered, built, and flew spy planes. More importantly for us, he spent his retirement applying his scientific

---

[iv] Examples taken from reference 12.
[v] From reference 8.

skills to putting, and in 1984, he published the first book on the science of putting.[vi] He explained that on a green with a consistent slope, all putts the same distance from the hole share a common *target point*.[vii] That is, we can aim any putt from the edge of a circle, which has the hole at its centre, at this single spot, and if we get the speed right, it will find the hole. The question is—where is it?

The target point is a spot on the green uphill from the hole, on the 'fall line' (Figure 4).[viii] The fall line is the line straight up and down the slope, on which a putt would have no break. If we poured water on the slope, it would run away down the fall line.

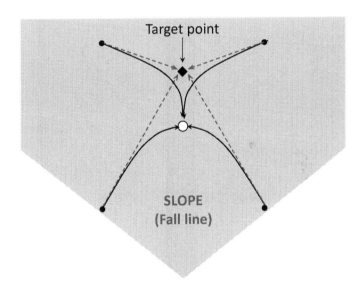

Figure 4. Common target point for equal length putts, on a sloping green.

[vi] 'Vector Putting'; reference 11.

[vii] Horace Templeton called it the *aim point*.

[viii] The target point isn't actually a point, it's a small, diamond-shaped area.

As putt length, slope, and green speed increase, the target point moves further up the fall line. Aiming at a point on the fall line is a new concept for many of us, because normally, we just aim left or right of the hole. But if we can adjust our thinking to uphill from the hole, we can use this remarkable slope geometry to improve our break reading.

It's a simple matter to find the target point for any putt, but we'd need two attempts. We aim our first putt straight at the hole, and putt to a dead length. We'd miss on the low side, but we can then measure the amount by which we missed, transfer it to the uphill side of the hole, on the fall line, and we have the correct target point for our second putt (Figure 5).

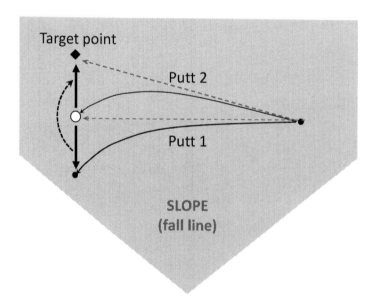

Figure 5. Calculating the target point using two putts.

Unfortunately, we're not allowed two putts, so we need to guess-timate it. We can work it out mathematically, if we know the exact slope angle, green speed, and putt distance,[ix] but most of us don't have these data, so we need a simpler method. Robert Grober, Professor of Physics at Yale University, has suggested a way of doing this. He suggests we assess not only the putt facing us, but also some imaginary putts of the same distance, a few paces to either side (Figure 6).[x]

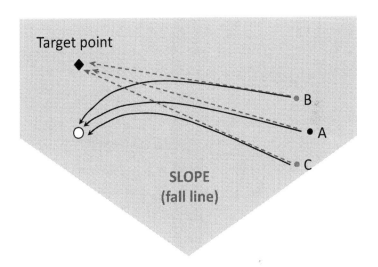

Figure 6. Common target point for three putts: the real putt (A), and two imaginary putts (B and C).

From the estimates taken from the real and imaginary putts, we can establish a common target point that feels right for all of them. We could walk a full circle around the hole, assessing many imaginary putts, and we'd come to a more accurate judgement, but it would take too long. Most of us look at putts from behind the ball and behind the hole anyway, so we already have two estimates. We

---

[ix] These calculations are the basis for the putting line that appears magically on our TV screens, before a player attempts a putt.
[x] Explained in detail in reference 2.

just need information from a few more. We'll see in Chapter 4 that our brains thrive on relevant information. The more we have, the better our judgement.[xi] This system offers an excellent blend of science and personal judgement. It gives us help from science, but allows our instincts and experience to make the final decision — always a good idea.

Before moving on, we should note that all of the above applies to *consistent* slopes. A consistent slope is flat, but inclined. Most slopes within 10–15 feet of the hole are consistent, but outside this range, things obviously get more complex.

So now, we've walked around, looked at the putt from various angles, and decided the best speed and line. Our next task is to address the ball, and *prepare* our stroke. During these final moments, we fine-tune our judgements, and create a *motor plan* that will generate a stroke to deliver the ball to the hole.[xii] In Part 2, we'll see how to do this, using our powers of *vision* and *imagery*.

\\/ \\/ \\/ I \\/ \\/ \\/

[xi] Note that our brains *don't* thrive on *irrelevant* information, which impairs our judgement. We'll cover this issue in Chapter 5.
[xii] A 'motor plan' is a signal package sent out by the brain to make the body move in a particular way. The signals trigger a series of muscular contractions that achieve a movement — for example, the putting stroke.

PUTTING KEYS

- We have a greater margin of error on downhill putts, compared to uphill putts.
- On a consistent slope, all putts the same distance from the hole share a common target point, uphill from the hole.
- Judging the target point using a range of (imaginary) putts is better than assessing only the real putt.

Part 2

Preparing the stroke

The time that we spend in studying the line of particular putts, long though it be, and infuriating to those who fume and fret in our immediate wake, is as nothing to that spent in wondering over the eternally baffling mystery of putting itself.

—Bernard Darwin, 1911

4

Vision

N EANDERTHALS DIED OUT AROUND 28,000 YEARS AGO, partly because they developed large eyes, to cope with the increased darkness they encountered as they trekked north out of Africa, towards Scandinavia. Having larger eyes meant they developed brains with greater visual processing capacity, so they had less brain available for other things, such as thinking. When the next ice age came, they couldn't work out a way to survive, and died out.[i] If Neanderthals had played golf, they would have been expert putters, because they had the perfect biological combination of great visual power, plus low thinking power—key ingredients of expert putting. We'll see in Chapter 7 that thinking damages our putting. Here, we'll see how *looking* at putts in the right way improves it.

---

[i] Strictly speaking, there wasn't a formal ice age at this time, just wild fluctuations of climate, especially temperature.

Visualisation

Jack Nicklaus always formulated a sharp, in-focus picture of every shot he planned. In putting, he explains it as seeing a movie of the ball rolling across the green and into the hole. We call this process *visualisation*.[ii] We all visualise, because it's our natural way of making judgements, but unfortunately, in putting, many of us do it badly.

Visualising the putt is the only way our brains can make sense of the massive amount of information we take in when we judge a putt: distance, slopes, grain, wetness/dryness, grass length, wind—even the presence of nearby lakes and hills.[iii] Each set of information is different, and we store them in layers inside our brains. Our brains then perform two remarkable feats.

First, they convert these disparate layers of information into a single image of a putt that will find the hole. Clearly, the ball will only find the hole if all layers are present and accurate, so if we miss any out, or get one wrong, we'll create a faulty image. Second, our brains convert the image into a motor plan for the stroke. We defined a motor plan earlier, but just to remind ourselves, it's a package of signals sent from the brain to the muscles, causing them to contract in sequence—the putting stroke. And if we get everything right, it will deliver the putt we imagined.

Our biggest problem – the reason we miss so many putts – is that we feed our brains too little *relevant* information, and too much *irrelevant* information. That is, we don't visualise correctly. Specifically, we don't look for long enough at the location that contains

---

[ii] In some texts, visualization is called *mental imagery*. They're the same thing.

[iii] Usually, land falls away from hills, and towards lakes.

virtually all the important information—the hole. Unfortunately, our brains can't judge the quality of the information they receive, they use everything, so looking at our hands, feet, spots on the green, and putterhead only serves to contaminate both the image and the motor plan. And flawed motor plans produce flawed putts—it's a case of 'garbage in, garbage out'. We can have a day of mechanically perfect putting, delivering all our putts to the wrong places.

We should also make sure that our image of the ball rolling across the green ends with it falling into the hole. This final, 'in the hole' image is important, because many studies have shown that players hole more putts when they visualise a holed putt, compared to visualising a miss. In one study, holding an image of a successful putt resulted in 50 percent more holed putts, compared with imaging a miss. This is important when we think back to Chapter 1, where we discussed how far past the hole to aim. While it's important to know how far past to aim, it's not a good idea to *visualise* the ball rolling past—we've missed. We should instead visualise the ball rolling into the hole at a speed that *would* take it to the desired distance should it miss.

It's clear that effective visualisation is a critical element of expert putting, so it's essential that we learn how to do it. The best way to approach this is to understand how our vision works, how it can sometimes fool us, and how we can make it work in our favour. First, we'll discuss some ways our vision can deceive us, then we'll move on to some practical ways in which we can harness its power. We'll start by considering why we sometimes see things bigger or smaller than they are.

Size counts

Unfortunately, when we take in visual information, our brains have a nasty habit of playing around with it, so we don't see things as they are. That is, we *perceive* things incorrectly. Here's a simple example, from handball, of how players try to take advantage of this human frailty.

If we look at the two straight lines in Figure 7, most of us will perceive the top line as longer than the bottom line. But they're the same length—we perceive them incorrectly.[iv] When facing a penalty, handball goalkeepers use this illusion to make themselves look bigger, filling the goal, and making the target areas look smaller (Figure 8).

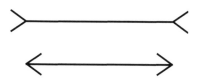

Figure 7. An optical illusion of two equal length lines.

Figure 8. The 'big' handball goalkeeping posture.

---

iv This is known as the *Muller-Lyer* illusion.

While this is a good example to show how perception works, it's not necessarily good news for the goalkeepers. Evidence suggests that having smaller target areas causes the penalty-takers to focus on the target more precisely, which creates a better motor plan, a better shot, and more goals. A better strategy would be for the goalkeepers to adopt a posture similar to the chevrons on the lower line, making themselves look smaller, by keeping their hands by their sides. This would encourage the penalty-taker to focus less precisely, create a flawed motor plan, and deliver a more central shot, which is easier to save. The takeaway message for our putting is that we mustn't have blind faith in our vision, because we can't always trust it. And one of our commonest flaws is to see a 'ghost hole' — we putt at a hole that isn't there.

The ghost hole

We see a ghost hole when we look at the hole, but see it in the wrong place. To be more precise, when we align the putterhead towards the hole, or target point, we can be fooled into aiming to the side, just enough to miss. Our problem is that we can only judge a straight line between two points when our eyes are in the same plane as both points. For example, assistant soccer referees can't judge offside unless they're looking straight across the pitch, in line with the most forward attacking player and the rearmost defender. If they're out of line, they don't have the visual information they need to judge a straight line.

We can make perceptual errors in our putting if we don't position our eyes vertically over the ball, because we won't see the putt in the same plane as the ball–hole line (Figure 9). If we position our eyes over our hands – a common position – we'll view the putt from inside the ball–target line, and we'll aim to the right. If our eyes are too far over the ball, we'll aim to the left. Rightward aiming errors are by far the most common. In fact, we even bump into objects on our right-hand side more often than objects on our left!

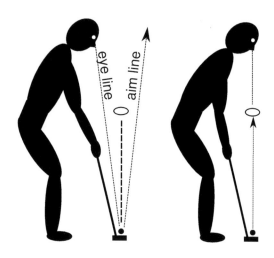

Figure 9. Effects of different eye positions on aim.

We can test whether we have an aiming problem. All we need is a putter, an aiming stick, and two golf balls. First, we can test our eye position by addressing one ball with our normal putting stance, and dropping the second ball from between our eyes. If it strikes the first ball dead centre, or left or right of centre, we have no problem, because our eyes are in the same plane as the ball. But if it lands inside or outside the first ball, we may have a problem.

Second, we can test our aim. We place the aiming stick on the ground, pointing roughly towards the hole, and take our normal putting stance. We then nudge the stick around with our putter until we perceive that it points at the hole. Finally, we walk behind the stick, and check. If it isn't pointing at the hole, we have an aiming error.

So this is the 'ghost hole': seeing the hole slightly to the right (usually) of where it actually is. We might now be tempted to go straight out onto the putting green, and practise getting our eyes over the ball. But we mustn't—this would be a mistake. Many of us putt without having our eyes over the ball, but we don't have an aiming problem. We've subconsciously cured the problem—we've *recalibrated*. Keegan Bradley, one of the world's best putters, has his eyes almost a foot inside the ball–target line, yet aims correctly.

Calibration is the reason we need to take both the tests described above. The important test is the second. Only if there's an aiming error should we consider adjusting our eye position. If there's no aiming error, changing our eye position will only make things worse. So, how does *calibration* work?

Calibration

Expert putters aim more accurately, compared to non-experts, but not because they position their eyes over the ball—they aim better because they're better calibrated. Our brains learn, via feedback from thousands of previous putts, how to correct subconsciously for aiming errors. We can see this in studies of golfers who have no aiming errors on their 'normal' (practised) side, but *do* have errors when they putt on their unpractised side (for example right-handed putters putting left-handed). Putting the wrong way round cancels out any calibration, and errors in eye position translate directly into aiming errors. The concept of calibration explains how, as we discussed earlier, we underestimate the effects of slopes on the ball's roll, yet manage to putt close to the correct line. Over time, we subconsciously recalibrate our stroke.

In practical terms, calibration means that although it's good to be aware of the effects of eye position, it's not always a good idea to change it. Anyone who plays and practises regularly will have recalibrated, and shouldn't change. The best way to check our level of calibration is to repeat the aiming test described earlier, but in reverse. First, we point the aiming stick exactly at the hole by aiming it from behind. We then take our normal stance (as if we were putting the stick), and check that we still perceive it as pointing at the hole. If we do, there's no problem. If we don't, we just need to adjust our eye position until we see the stick pointing at the hole. Alternatively, we can simply aim the ball's logo from behind, and then forget all about it.

Putting to bigger holes

Basketball star Lebron James, who plays forward for the Miami Heat, describes scoring baskets during a hot shooting streak as "as easy as throwing tennis balls into the ocean".[v] And in sports that involve striking small, moving balls, such as cricket, tennis, or baseball, players say they "see it like a football" on good hitting days. In golf, we've all heard of, or experienced, the perception that the hole looks bigger when we're putting well. We say that the hole "looks like a bucket" on good putting days, and we talk about eggcups on bad days.

This isn't our imagination, it's a real effect. In one study, researchers asked players, after their round, to choose the correct hole

---

[v] Taken from an interview broadcast by CNN; February, 2013.

size from a series of different-sized circles drawn on a sheet of paper. Players who scored lower that day chose bigger holes.[vi] There's a strong relationship between putting performance and perceived hole size. Interestingly, there's no relationship between handicap and perceived hole size, so the important factor isn't how good a putter we are generally—it's how good we are *today*.

We can improve our putting by making this illusion happen. We can make the hole look bigger by looking at it for longer. Looking at the hole for longer gives our brains extra relevant information, plus additional processing time, so we see the hole as bigger, create a better motor plan, and deliver a better putt. And, as we might expect, looking at irrelevant locations – virtually everything except the hole – destroys the effect.

Until recently, this was a chicken and egg situation, because we weren't sure whether holing putts causes the hole to look bigger, or whether seeing a bigger hole results in more holed putts. Or both. This is important, because if it's the first case, it means we can't train the effect. We need to putt well first (somehow), and then we'll see the bigger holes. But recent evidence suggests the opposite— seeing bigger holes leads to more holed putts. The important evidence comes from studies where researchers made equal-sized holes appear bigger or smaller, using special lighting. Players consistently putted more accurately towards the holes that appeared bigger.[vii]

Seeing bigger or smaller holes explains why our putting form tends to go in streaks and slumps. We love streaks, because we get into a wonderful cycle of holing a few putts, seeing bigger holes,

---

vi Taken from reference 63.
vii Taken from reference 64.

holing more putts, and so on. Unfortunately, slumps are equally common, as we miss a few putts, see smaller holes, and miss more putts.

Clearly, the important message for our putting is—look more at the hole, and less at everything else. And when we're a long way from the hole, or it's hardly visible over a hump, we can always revert to that old-fashioned method of asking our caddie or companion to 'attend the flag'. A flag we can see is always better than a hole we can't.

Next, we come to a visual problem that confuses many of us: how to putt at the hole, while looking at the ball. In other words, what's the best way to divide our visual attention between the hole and the ball? We need to learn how to *gaze*.

> *Talent hits a target no one else can hit; genius hits a target no one else can see.*[viii]

—Arthur Schopenhauer, German philosopher

PUTTING KEYS

ɪ We combine our judgements of speed and line by visualising the putt we intend.

ɪ Our brains convert this image into a motor plan, which produces a stroke to deliver the imagined putt.

ɪ We can't rely on our perception of any putt—we need to check our aiming skill, and our level of calibration.

ɪ Looking at the hole makes it appear bigger, and leads to better putts.

5

Gaze

WE WERE PROBABLY ALL TOLD AS CHILDREN to 'keep our eye on the ball' in order to hit or catch it. This is excellent advice, because a moving ball is difficult to deal with. In putting, we have a different problem: we need to look at the ball in order to strike it accurately, but putt it towards a target we can't see. In other words, we have both *far* and *near* targets to deal with, and we need a strategy for dividing our attention between the two.

Looking at the hole gives us important information on speed and line, whereas looking at the ball promotes accurate putter-ball contact, so we need to look at both. But we have one huge advantage: the ball is stationary, so we hardly need look at it at all. This means we can look at the hole – which contains all the important information – as much as we want. How we divide our attention between the hole and the ball is called our *gaze pattern*.

Gaze patterns

In any precision aiming sport, the longer we gaze at the target, the higher our chances of hitting it. We can take an example from soccer. Soccer goalkeepers save more penalty kicks when they adopt a steady gaze – called a *fixation* – at the ball. And at the other end of the penalty, penalty-takers who gaze longer at their chosen target – normally a corner of the goal – before the run up, score more goals.[i]

Goalkeepers can disrupt the gaze patterns of penalty-takers, as happened in the 1984 European Cup final between Liverpool and Roma, which was decided by a penalty shoot-out. At a crucial point, when the penalty scores were level, Liverpool goalkeeper Bruce Grobbelaar pretended his legs had lost strength, and he was falling to the ground. Grobbelaar's antics – known as his 'spaghetti legs' routine – attracted the penalty-taker's gaze, resulting in a terrible shot that went over the bar. Liverpool won.[ii]

In putting, longer gazes at the hole lead to better putts. Whenever we look away from the hole, we stop processing relevant information, and waste time. Worse still, if we gaze at irrelevant things, we process *contaminating* information, which nullifies the gazing at the hole we've done already. We need to look at the hole—and for longer than many of us do at present.

We can obtain important clues about effective gaze patterns from putting experts. Experts have fewer, longer fixations, mostly on the hole, with the rest on the ball. They focus on the hole early, and transfer their gaze swiftly between the hole and the ball. They tend not to gaze anywhere else. As TV commentators say, they "stare

---

[i] England soccer team, please note ….
[ii] A video of Grobbelaar's spaghetti legs routine can be seen on YouTube: http://www.youtube.com/watch?v=A2WCKXICGd0

down the hole" (like a Tiger …). Finally, they fixate for 1–2 seconds on the ball before they start the stroke. In contrast, the gaze of non-experts switches randomly between many locations, most of which are irrelevant to the putt. In particular, they look at the hole too little, and the ball too much.

Not only do we need to look at the hole for longer, we also need to look at it precisely, because we have only a small field of vision in which everything's in focus—just three degrees (Figure 10). This is about the width of a thumb held out vertically at arm's length. At 10 feet, it's around 4 inches wide—the size of the hole. Outside this narrow field, things are out-of-focus, because they're in our 'peripheral vision'. Peripheral vision detects movement, and can't provide any clear, visual information. Note that while reading these words we focus on one word, and the words to either side are out of focus.

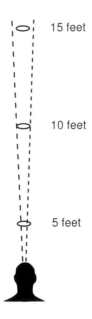

Figure 10. Three-degree field of focus at distances of 5, 10, and 15 feet.

The clear message for our putting is that we need to take long looks at the hole, and only brief looks at the ball in between. And for short putts, we need to look at a small part of the hole, for example, the centre of the far rim. It will come with training. Our eyes will soon learn to ignore the putterhead (once we've aimed it), spots on the green, hands, feet, and all the other things that distract us.

Interestingly, there's good evidence that looking at the *hole* while we putt is just as effective as looking at the ball! No matter how much we don't want to believe this – because it just feels wrong – it's at least worth a try on the lounge carpet ....

Now, having looked at the hole (a lot), and the ball (a bit), we've gathered all the relevant information, and we're almost ready to start the stroke. But not quite. We need to perform one simple, final task. We need to ensure that when our gaze returns to the ball for the final time, we look at it for the right amount of time, before starting the stroke. The timing of this final gaze at the ball is crucial to the putt—it's the start of the *quiet eye period*.

The quiet eye period

The Rev. Dr. David R. Adamovich is a sports scientist with a doctorate in exercise physiology from Columbia University. But his contribution to putting isn't through sports science—it's through knife throwing. David Adamovich gave up the academic life to become *The Great Throwdini*—the world's fastest knife thrower. Throw (as he's known to his friends) can hurl two knives per second into a revolving board (the 'double-veiled wheel of death'), missing two target girls strapped across it.[iii] Throw can also catch knives, holding the world record of 25 successful catches in one minute.[iv] What's important for us is that knife throwing demands an effective *quiet eye period*, because it makes the difference between hits and misses—in Throw's case, between life and death. And when catching knives, it's important to catch the handle.

> *Catching the knife, I have to watch that knife coming toward*
> *me ... I watch the release very carefully as it leaves the*
> *thrower's hand ...*

—The Great Throwdini, July 2010[v]

At the time of writing, more than 700 academic articles investigating the quiet eye period have been published. Mostly, these are clinical studies, investigating the effectiveness of quiet eye training in teaching physically impaired patients to make accurate movements. But during the last 15 years, more than 100 research papers have appeared, investigating the role of quiet eye in precision aiming and striking sports, including darts, football, tennis, basketball, baseball, shooting, billiards, and golf. The important point for us is that golfers who have optimal quiet eye periods hole more putts.

The quiet eye period is our final fixation on the ball, and lasts from the moment our gaze returns to the ball for the final time until

---

[iii] Those of a ghoulish inclination can see this performance at http://www.youtube.com/watch?v=a6Rl00wzR98.

[iv] While trying to break this record, Throw made an unsuccessful catch, and the attempt came to a bloody halt.

[v] Extracted from a 'Big Think' interview transcript.

just after impact. It acts like a GPS system, feeding three-dimensional putt coordinates into the brain, which then plots the perfect putterhead route.[vi] Using this information, the brain fine-tunes the motor plan for a putting action that has appropriate force, direction, balance, timing, and control. In short, it ensures the best possible putt. The quiet eye period is effective because it implants information on the hole's location more accurately into the motor plan. It gives the brain the optimum amount of time – neither too little nor too much – to formulate the best possible plan.

When we make a putting stroke, our brains need to organise more than 100 billion neurons into appropriate neural networks, which contract dozens of muscles controlling our hands, arms, and body throughout the stroke. These temporary networks are the motor plan, and they develop gradually, while we prepare the putt. The optimum plan occurs a second or two after our gaze leaves the hole for the final time, and the networks will only stay organized for a few moments. This means we have a brief time window in which to catch the best plan, and make the best stroke. We don't want to putt through the window before it's fully open, nor while it's closing. The quiet eye period ensures we catch it at the best possible time—when it's fully open.

We've obtained much of the evidence for quiet eye through studying the gaze patterns of experts in a range of high-skill sports. In rock climbing, a longer final gaze at the next hold promotes a more accurate reaching and grasping movement. Shotgun (skeet) shooters have earlier onset, and longer duration, quiet eye periods before successful shots. And in golf, expert putters have longer quiet eye

---

[vi] GPS = Global Positioning System.

periods, compared to non-experts—double the length. The importance of quiet eye extends beyond sport, with surgeons trained in quiet eye being more accurate than surgeons trained technically.

In terms of our putting, we need to know the precise timings within the quiet eye period. When we return our gaze to the ball for the final time, how long should we wait, before we start the stroke?

Duration of quiet eye

First, let's remind ourselves when the quiet eye period starts, and when it stops. It starts the moment we return our gaze from the hole to the ball for the final time, and it stops a fraction of a second after impact. We should also remind ourselves that the quiet eye period has an *optimum* length. It can be too short, and too long.

For successful billiards shots, players have quiet eye periods averaging 0.4 seconds for easy shots, 0.6 seconds for difficult shots, and 1.2 seconds for very difficult shots. When they miss, quiet eye periods are much shorter, at 0.2–0.4 seconds. In shotgun shooting, quiet eye periods for successful shots are around 0.5 seconds, and again, much shorter for misses.

In putting, quiet eye periods are longer, because the stroke itself takes longer. In expert putters, quiet eye periods last around 2.5 seconds: one second before the stroke starts, one second during the stroke, and up to half a second after impact.[vii] Joan Vickers, Professor of Kinesiology at the University of Calgary, an expert in quiet eye, advises that the optimum duration of the quiet eye period in putting is 2–3 seconds, depending on putt difficulty.[viii]

[vii] Taken from reference 55.
[viii] Personal communication from Professor Joan Vickers.

The most important timing is the one-second gaze at the ball, before we start the stroke. Some of us start the stroke as soon as we see the ball, because we're concerned we might lose information about the hole. But we can retain the information for a second or two after looking away. We can 'see it with our third eye', a virtual eye in the side of our head. But after a few seconds, the third eye starts to close, and the information starts to deteriorate. There are others among us who stare interminably at the ball, rehearsing how we're going to swing the putter. Be warned: this *will* result in lost information, and bad putts.

Quiet eye under pressure

When we depart from our normal gaze pattern and/or quiet eye period, putting accuracy deteriorates, and the most likely time for this to happen is when we're under pressure. For some reason, pressure makes us look in all the wrong places. For example, when high on a rock face, climbers have more frequent, shorter gazes at more locations: the rope, the rock, their hands, the top of the climb, even down! Compare this with lower down the climb, where their gaze is fixed, confident, and steady on the next hold. In other words, rock climbers 'choke' under pressure, because their gaze patterns and quiet eye periods disintegrate.[ix]

There's very little in the world of sport that causes more pressure than a short, important putt, so choking is common on the putting green. A putting stroke under pressure looks 'steery', because we're trying to steer the ball deliberately, searching for extra control. The stroke becomes either too slow and deliberate, or short and

---

[ix] 'Choking' is a breakdown in skill when under pressure.

jabby. Our problem is, we're trying too hard. We take extra time, extra looks, and adopt extra thoughts. But we shouldn't, we should maintain our normal routine. In putting, even though our tendency under pressure is to look everywhere, trying to be extra careful, we need to maintain our normal gaze pattern if we want to hole the putt. We'll discuss pressure and choking more fully in Chapter 7, and the problems of trying too hard in Chapter 9.

Training quiet eye

The important issue is whether we can train our gaze patterns, and improve our putting. And the answer is yes. We have abundant evidence from many sports, including putting, that simple visual training techniques generate instant and sustained improvements. For example, after quiet eye training, soccer penalty-takers directed the ball three ball-widths further away from the goalkeeper, leading to 50 percent fewer saves.[x] Quiet eye training in basketball players resulted in field shooting accuracy improving from 46 to 61 percent. In shotgun shooters, the percentage of successful shots increased from 62 to 70 percent after quiet eye training.

These improvements are huge, and luckily, golfers of all abilities respond equally well to training. Novice golfers receiving quiet eye training showed greater putting improvement, compared to novices receiving instruction on correct mechanics. And low-handicap golfers (average handicap 2.7) holed 50 percent more 10-foot putts after quiet eye training, with missed putts finishing 50 percent closer to the hole. Importantly, the improvements transferred from

---

[x] England soccer team, again, *please* take note ....

the laboratory to the golf course—during competition, these already good putters took an average of two putts fewer per round.[xi]

Quiet eye training for putting can be complicated, involving vision experts, sophisticated eye measurements, and complex gaze-tracking equipment. Or it can be simple, involving nothing more than practising looking at the right things at the right time. We can make considerable progress with our putting if we practise the optimum gaze pattern (Figure 11).

1.	Longer gazes at the hole;
2.	Brief gazes at the ball;
3.	No gazes at the clubhead, after aiming;
4.	A final, longer gaze at the ball of 1.0–1.5 seconds;
5.	Gaze stays on the ball, then the green beneath the ball, until at least 0.2 seconds (one blink of an eye) after impact;
6.	Total quiet eye period of 2.5–3.0 seconds, depending on putt difficulty.

Figure 11. The optimum gaze pattern for putting.[xii]

A final refinement to our gaze strategy for any breaking putt is to fixate on the ball's entry point to the hole (Figure 12). This is an excellent way of linking our image of the putt with our gaze strategy. With increasing slope steepness, the entry point shifts further to the high side of the hole.

[xi] Data taken from reference 56.
[xii] Compiled from various elite protocols.

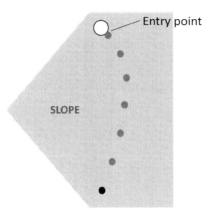

Figure 12. Entry point to the hole for a breaking putt.

So now, we've gathered all the relevant information, absorbed it, converted it into a motor plan, and fine-tuned the plan through an effective quiet eye period. All that remains is to swing the putter according to the plan. The question now is whether the motor plan will deliver a stroke with sound mechanical fundamentals. We've arrived at the *putting stroke* itself.

> *I know one enthusiastic player – an admirable holer-out at a*
> *pinch – who declares that he can hole any putt if he only looks*
> *at it long enough.*

—Bernard Darwin, 1911

PUTTING KEYS

1 Effective gaze patterns are critical to good putting.

1 An effective gaze pattern includes longer gazes at the hole, shorter gazes at the ball, and no gazes anywhere else.

1 The final gaze at the ball is the start of the quiet eye period, which lasts 2–3 seconds.

1 An effective quiet eye period reduces the risk of choking on pressure putts.

1 We can improve gaze patterns and quiet eye periods through vision training.

Part 3

The stroke

The putt of the average golfer is only worthy of the name of a little hit, but the putt of a good putter is a stroke.

—Bernard Darwin, 1911

6

Stroke mechanics

W E CAN MEASURE STROKE MECHANICS ACCURATELY, using high-tech imaging and sensing equipment. We can measure body positions and movements, such as posture, weight distribution, balance, grip pressure, alignment, head movement, and the strength of muscular contractions. We can also measure putterhead movements, such as speed, acceleration, path, face angle, and the quality of putter-ball contact (known as *impact conditions*). This technology, combined with important evidence from physics, biomechanics, and neuroscience, has revealed three key components of an effective stroke:

- Putterhead path (and face angle);
- Stroke tempo;
- Control of path and tempo.

Putterhead path

Here, we're interested in both the putterhead path, and changes in its face angle during the stroke. Putterhead path determines around 20 percent of the initial ball direction, whereas face angle determines virtually all the remaining 80 percent. Off-centre hits cause small errors in both distance and direction, but they're negligible, at less than one percent. This means that although this is a 'putterhead path' section, changes in face angle are actually more important. But the two are related, so for practical purposes, we can deal with them together.

We can start with the perfect theoretical putterhead path. Complex computer simulations have determined a putterhead motion that satisfies the scientific criteria for an accurate mechanical movement:

- ⟁ The putterhead stays vertically above the ball–target line from address to impact;
- ⟁ The face stays square to the ball–target line from address to impact (Figure 13).[i]

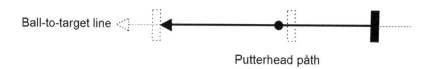

Figure 13. The perfect theoretical putterhead path.

---

[i] Taken from reference 71.

To achieve this putterhead path, we need to perform two body movements:

- Move the arms away from the body on the backswing, and towards the body on the downswing;
- Rotate the forearms anticlockwise on the backswing, and clockwise on the downswing.

The problem is, to produce this mechanically optimal stroke, we need to make two distinctly sub-optimal movements. Deliberately separating our arms from our bodies, and rotating our forearms in the 'wrong' direction, are both unnatural movements, so although this technique may produce the purest mechanical swing, it's difficult.[ii]

This leads us to the view that the optimal putting stroke isn't the best mechanical solution, but the best biological solution. That is, the swing we can *control* most easily, within the limitations of human anatomy. We can confirm this is the case when we analyse the putterhead paths of experts. Less than five percent of tournament professionals use the stroke described above, whereas ninety-five percent use a more natural, anatomically suitable stroke:

- The putterhead travels slightly inside the ball–target line during the backswing;
- The face angle – the angle between the putterface and the ball–target line – opens between one and two degrees (Figure 14).

[ii] In the full golf swing, we do the opposite: we avoid separating our arms from our bodies, and our forearms rotate *clockwise* during the backswing, and *anticlockwise* during the downswing.

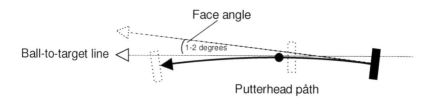

Figure 14. The optimal human putterhead path.

With respect to the change in face angle, we should note that although the face opens in relation to the ball–target line, it *doesn't* open in relation to the swing path—it stays square. This is important, because it means we *don't* achieve the change in face angle by rotating our forearms—it's a natural result of our shoulders rotating on an inclined plane. And because it's not a forced movement, we reverse it equally naturally during the downswing. We don't need to worry about how much inside the line the putterhead travels, nor how much the face angle changes, because they'll be different for all of us. We just need to allow these movements to happen, following the natural swing we make with our shoulders and arms.

Now, we have a mental picture of where the putterhead should go. Our next problem is to find the best *tempo*.

Putterhead tempo

Tempo refers to changes in putterhead speed and acceleration through the stroke, and our purpose here is to identify if there's an optimum tempo. There is—and we might be a little surprised to discover what it is. In order to understand tempo, we need to consider how any system – for example, our putting stroke – moves.

Every system has a set of conditions within which it moves most freely, called its *natural frequency*.[iii] In these conditions, even small forces acting on the system cause large movements. In some systems, this can lead to disaster, as was the case with 'Galloping Gertie', the original Tacoma Narrows Bridge in Washington State. During windy conditions, the bridge vibrated and twisted wildly, hence its nickname. On November 7th 1940, the wind caused the bridge to vibrate exactly at its natural frequency, and it moved and twisted so much that it broke apart, collapsing into the river below. In the case of a bridge, we don't want it to find its natural frequency.

But in other systems, we do, because the ability to apply small forces and cause large system movements is a big advantage. For example, when pushing a child on a swing, we can find a pushing rhythm that fits the swing's natural frequency, so we only need to apply gentle pushes to keep the child swinging happily. Similarly, we find spinning a hula-hoop around our hips easier when we find the rhythm of hip gyration that fits the hoop's natural frequency. Smaller hoops need faster hips.

In putting, we have a dilemma, because we want to putt at the smooth rhythm of a child's swing – a simple pendulum – but we *don't* want small forces to cause large system movements. That is, we don't want small stroke errors to translate into large putterhead errors. But if we putt at the even-paced, tick-tock rhythm of a simple pendulum – the putting swing's natural frequency – they will. This even-paced tempo may look fluid and smooth, but it's deceptively hard to control, because the putterhead tends to 'wander', under the influence of small errors we make in our stroke.

[iii] The technical term is *resonant frequency*.

Luckily, there's a way to overcome this problem. We can maintain a smooth stroke, *and* protect our stroke from unwanted forces, if we swing the putter at a multiple of the stroke's natural frequency. We could choose double, or treble, or even more. In practical terms, the optimal putting tempo – one that is rhythmical, resistant to outside forces, and feels natural – is *double* the tempo of a simple pendulum. Professor Robert Grober has again described the detailed physics of a double-tempo stroke, but here, we only need concern ourselves with two things: what it is, and how to do it.[iv]

The double-tempo stroke

In a simple pendulum, swinging at its natural frequency, the upswings take the same time as the downswings. In a double-tempo putting stroke, the backswing takes double the time of the downswing, which we achieve by driving the downswing harder. Our stroke becomes a *driven* pendulum.

Most expert putters do this. They've found a ratio of backswing to downswing time averaging 2.0—double tempo.[v] An expert's backswing takes 0.6–0.8 seconds, compared to the downswing, which takes 0.3–0.4 seconds. In non-experts, the ratio is closer to one, where the backswings and downswings take equal time, around 0.5 seconds each. The key difference between experts and non-experts isn't one of speed – as is commonly believed – it's one of tempo. It's tick-tick-tock, not tick-tock.

[iv] References 78 and 79 contain the detailed physics.
[v] Note that this is the ratio of *times* taken for the backswing and downswing. We shouldn't confuse this with the 'stroke:length ratio', which is the ratio of *distances* moved during the backswing and downswing.

An important feature of the double-tempo stroke is the need for a shorter backswing, combined with a longer follow through. Again, this is what expert putters do. Figure 15 shows the backswing and downswing paths of experts and non-experts for different length putts.

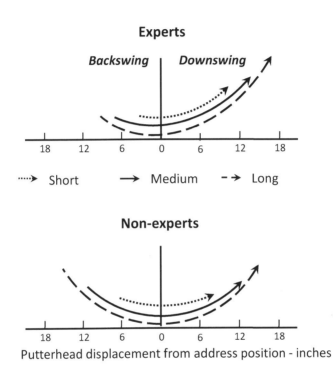

Figure 15. *Putterhead paths for short-, medium-, and long-range putts: experts and non-experts.*[vi]

Note how the experts take shorter backswings – around 50 percent shorter – and longer follow-throughs. It's a more positive strike at the ball. Note that this isn't a throwback to 'rap' putting, popular in the 1960s, and characterised by Gary Player. Rap putting

---

[vi] Diagram based on data from reference 91.

also involved a driven downswing, but the putterhead stopped just after impact.

We should also note that in the experts' double-tempo stroke, the total time of the stroke stays the same, irrespective of putt length. For longer putts, they take longer swings, but they also drive the stroke harder. Annex 1 contains practices that will encourage a double-tempo stroke, using simple counting sequences.

Before we leave the issue of tempo, we should address a question that sometimes causes confusion: whether we should *accelerate* the putterhead through the ball. That is, should we apply force to the putter throughout the downswing right up to, and beyond, impact? Again, we can see what expert putters do. Expert putters achieve a constant putterhead speed at impact, with zero acceleration. They've acquired the skill of applying the correct amount of force early in the downswing, and then relaxing through impact. So the answer is no.

Now, having discovered the best putterhead path and tempo, we can turn to the question of how to achieve them. We know what we want the putterhead to do, and all the correct timings, but how can we make it all happen? In other words, how do we establish precise *putterhead control?*

Controlling path and tempo

When considering the best way to make a putting stroke, it's tempting to discuss things such as posture, grip, head position, alignment, weight distribution, wrist angles, and shoulder movements. But we have no evidence that any of these affects either putterhead control or putting accuracy. For example, it's been shown that the normal grip performs just as well as cross-handed or split-handed grips; wide and narrow stances are equally effective in maintaining balance; putting with some weight shift works just as well as keeping the body still. We also have no objective evidence that putter design has any influence, with blade, mallet, and winged putterhead designs all performing pretty much the same. So we can take that latest putter – the one with the 'trampoline-effect drumhead striking surface and pendulum plumb-bob peripheral weight distribution' (it exists …) – off our Christmas lists.

And this fits with the science, because – it's worth repeating – controlling a motor skill isn't a body or an equipment problem— it's a *brain* problem. To control the putterhead, we need to *think* correctly. We have decades of research to show this. We'll achieve precise putterhead control not by adopting any specific collection of mechanical techniques, but by using our innate, biological control systems. This is where neuroscience – especially the new brain-imaging equipment – becomes so important. We've learnt a huge amount about how to control a putting stroke since we gained the ability to see what's going on in a player's brain during the stroke. We can actually see the control systems at work. These systems are our most powerful weapon, but in many of us, they remain an untapped resource.

The best way to explain how these systems control our stroke is to consider the two schools of thought regarding putterhead control. One school focuses on *restricting movement* as much as possible. We putt like a robot. The second school allows some *freedom of movement*. We putt like a human. There's a clue here—we're humans, not robots.

Robot putting

If we're in the robotic school, we believe in rigidity. We freeze as many joints as possible, trying to restrict the number of moving parts, and prevent movement 'errors' from creeping in. When we make a putting error, we believe we allowed ourselves to unfreeze. Robot putting is an attractive model, because we know that putting robots don't miss, and they have only a small number of rigid, moving parts.

We're even more convinced of the robotic model when we look at human anatomy. We see a collection of limbs, joined by highly flexible joints that can all move in many directions, operated by hundreds of muscles all working in different ways. We don't like this at all. We think that such a flexible, wobbly body can't putt like a robot. So we try to be robots.

Interestingly, this is the opposite of how we approach the full golf swing. In the full swing, beginners freeze as many joints as possible, trying to limit the number of things that can go wrong. With practice and good coaching, they learn to 'free up' their joints, producing more fluid, well-controlled swings. There's no reason to approach putting any differently.

Human putting

The obvious problem with robotic putting is that we're not robots. We have flexible bodies, because we need to perform many complicated movements, such as brushing teeth, texting, walking, and washing dishes. Our flexibility enables us to do these things, and we've developed highly effective systems to control the complex movements. In contrast, a putting robot only has one job—putting. An engineer will therefore construct a robot to be rigid and mechanical, and to obey the laws of physics. Humans are built from flesh and bones—we obey the laws of motor control. In other words, robotic putting swings are best for robots; fluid swings are best for humans. We shouldn't mix them up.

The crucial point is that we can exert precise putterhead control *because* we have flexible bodies. The freedom of movement in our joints *is* the control mechanism. In short, humans perform high-level motor skills not by freezing the body, but by *freeing* it. In the human school, our flexible joints work together, continually compensating and correcting, stabilising the putterhead motion. These subtle movements give the stroke the smoothness and fluidity that we see in expert putters.

Free putting

In putting, the robotic approach dominates, and has done for some time. If we look around the practice putting green at a golf tournament, we'll see an amazing array of postures, grips, putters, alignment mats, mirrors, plane trainers, path trainers, chalked strings, putting rails, lasers, and metronomes. The overall impression is that everyone is trying to *exert* control over the putterhead, trying to make it behave. Only a few players are *allowing* control to happen, trusting their instinctive control systems to guide the stroke.

Most of this effort to exert control goes against the science of improving a motor skill. It also goes against the evidence of what makes an expert putter. For example, we know that players who have variable strokes putt more accurately than players who have rigid, invariable strokes. The best putters don't swing the putter identically every time, but they produce almost identical impact conditions for each stroke. Non-experts have more deliberate, inflexible swings, which produce inconsistent impact conditions, and less accurate putts.

The key point is that we can cope with deviations from 'perfect', caused by unintended forces we apply. We have a funnel-shaped control mechanism that corrects errors throughout the stroke, reducing them to a minimum at impact. We subconsciously correct an unwanted movement in one joint by making compensatory movements in nearby joints, bringing *overall* stability to the most important thing—the putterhead.[vii]

This calls into question the wisdom of thinking of the putting stroke as a pendulum. We may be better to compare it with an aeroplane's automatic landing system. As a plane descends towards the runway, the on-board computer collects a stream of information, comparing progress with the pre-programmed descent path. The computer analyses the information, and makes continual fine adjustments to the plane's speed and direction, so that it finds the runway. Similarly, in putting, we pre-programme our brains with the putterhead's flight plan – our motor plan – and the brain monitors progress, applying small corrections. This is the essence of controlling any motor skill. In putting, we need to free up those rigid pendulums. Just a little ….

Now that we understand how to control the putterhead, we need to ensure that our guidance systems operate at maximum effectiveness. And excitingly, we don't need to do anything, because they'll happen automatically. They're instinctive, so we just need to ensure we don't stifle them. And we do this by adopting a *quiet mind*.

[vii] This scientific field of study, which integrates the biomechanics of movement with the neuroscience of movement control, is called *dynamic systems*.

PUTTING KEYS

❧ During the backswing, the optimum putterhead path is slightly inside the ball-target line, accompanied by a slight opening of the face angle.

❧ Expert putters have double-tempo strokes, in which the backswing takes double the time of the downswing.

❧ Allowing some freedom of movement in our joints allows our subconscious control mechanisms to exert precise putterhead control.

7

A quiet mind

zzz ...

MANY OF US WILL HAVE HEARD, just before we attempt an important putt, that most overused, vague – yet well intentioned – word of advice: "*Concentrate* …". The problem with concentrating is that we don't know what to concentrate on, so mostly, we just concentrate on concentrating.

But there's a science behind what to think about while we're making a putting stroke—and it tells us we should think about as little as possible. In recent years, a number of authors have published texts on what we might call 'putting without thinking about it', and we don't need to repeat the information here. But we do need to know how it works, why it's so important, and how we can build it into our scientific putting framework.

In terms of performing a motor skill, the human brain is both highly competent, and severely limited. Specifically, it's highly competent at performing skills *subconsciously*, and falls apart when it tries to perform them *consciously*. In other words, our brains perform a physical skill most effectively when they're not thinking about how to do it. This chapter explains how thinking about technique destroys our putting strokes, whereas thinking about virtually anything else produces our best strokes. It's a short story, involving brainwaves, automaticity, choking, the 'yips', and Kim Basinger. The best place to start is with *alpha brainwaves*.

Alpha waves

In all precision aiming sports, a calm and relaxed mind in the moments before and during the shot is a powerful predictor of whether we hit the target or not. Only when our brains are calm do our bodies pull triggers, shoot arrows, and swing putters accurately. We can measure these effects. We can detect different brainwave patterns before successful and unsuccessful shots and putts. Specifically, we can detect differences in *alpha waves*.

Alpha waves indicate stillness, calm, and relaxed concentration—perfect for putting. We need a calm brain when we putt, not a brain that's trying hard. *High* alpha activity is associated with *low* brain activity, so we need lots of alpha waves when we putt. The stronger the alpha, the more accurate the putt.

Most of us know that a calm mind produces better putts, but we may not know that we need the calmness in our *left* brains. We've probably read about how our left and right brains do different things: our left brain is logical; our right brain is creative. Figure 16 lists some of the more important functions of each side.

Uses logic   Uses feeling
Attends to details   Sees the big picture
Likes facts   Likes to imagine
Deals in words and language   Deals in symbols and images
Sees order and patterns   Sees space and dimensions

Figure 16. Main functions of the left and right brains.

Unfortunately, the left–right brain distinction is frequently exaggerated – sometimes wildly – when it's applied to real life situations. Despite what we may have read, we're not, as individuals, either 'left brained' or 'right-brained'. While we may have tendencies to favour one way of thinking over the other, we use both sides of our brain all the time. The two sides communicate, and work together on most everyday tasks. In fact, if we injure one side of our brain, the other side will compensate, taking over many of its roles.[i]

In putting, we need both sides of the brain to be involved at different times—the crucial thing is when. Essentially, we need to use our logical left brains when we judge speed and line, then we need to calm them down, allowing our right brains to dominate the stroke. We should devote those last few moments standing over the putt to calming the left brain, and allowing the right brain to take over. It may be that the quiet eye period works so well in sport because it enables this left-to-right shift in activity to take place, ensuring optimal mental conditions for performing the skill.

We can see the effects of brain activity on performance in other sports. In a study of expert archers, high left-brain alpha (low brain

---

[i] We call this *brain plasticity.*

activity) during the final three seconds of aiming consistently predicted successful shots. Alpha activity was even higher during the final one second, and higher still during the final half second. The archers clearly shot best when they achieved a strong, left to right shift in brain activity, calming the left brain, and activating the right brain. We see similar effects in shooting. Expert shooters sometimes reject a shot. They don't pull the trigger. They lower the gun, and start again, because they say "it doesn't feel right". Rejected shots are preceded by low left-brain alpha (high brain activity) — the opposite of what's required.

In our world of putting, effective left-to-right shifts in brain activity lead to more holed putts. In fact, of all the sports studied, we see the strongest effects in putting. And the key to achieving a left-to-right transition is to avoid *thinking*, because thinking is a logical, left-brain activity. We activate our left brains whenever we need to work something out, or deal with something complicated, so it's ideal for calculating speed and line. But once we take our stance over the ball, any left-brain activity harms the stroke, so at this point, we need to stop thinking logically. Specifically, we need to avoid thinking about technique, or talking to ourselves. This may explain why imaging the putt is so effective — it stops us being too logical about our putting stroke.

Most of us will have experienced the effects of an unexpected noise or movement just as we're about to putt. The interruption wakes up our left brain, which we're trying to calm down. If it occurs while we're weighing up the putt, it doesn't matter, because we're using our left brain anyway, and a little extra activity isn't a problem. But if it occurs in those final few seconds before we putt, it short-circuits the left-to-right transition of brain activity — in fact, it reverses it. We need to stand up, walk away, and start over. Note that a constant, background noise, or movement – such as traffic, birds singing, or crowd movements – isn't too much of a problem, but unexpected noises and movements are. We could use this to our advantage while our opponent is putting—but of course, we won't.

There are clear links between this pre-performance period of relaxed calm, and the concept of *flow*, an elusive state of effortless concentration that sportsmen and women sometimes experience before and during a great performance. They speak about 'being in the zone', a state of focused attention, immune to outside interference. Expert artists, golfers, musicians, surgeons, chess players, and rock climbers report a single common feature of flow—a feeling of *automaticity*. A sense that the 'piano is playing itself'. This happens in putting—the best strokes make themselves, as we'll see shortly.

Our task now is to discover how to achieve this calm, relaxed state, and we'll see that it depends entirely on what we think about during the stroke. We obviously need to think about something, and in putting, we make our best strokes when we adopt an *external focus of attention*.

External and internal focus

Golf writer Dan Jenkins, when reflecting on how complex we've made the golf swing, often refers to his golf instruction book: 'How to play relatively good golf, while thinking about Kim Basinger'. The book may or may not exist, but whether Dan knows it or not, the title captures the scientific essence of what we should think about to produce our best putting strokes. The important point is that an image of Kim Basinger is a long way removed from stroke mechanics.

We have a choice of what to think about when we putt. Some of us think about technique, a logical, left-brain activity that directs focus *internally* to the body. Others think of, for example, the hole, or the ball rolling towards the hole, which has nothing to do with technique, and is *external* to the body. The internal focusers will be worse putters, because internal focus damages the stroke's *automaticity*. With practice, we automate our putting strokes, which is a huge advantage, but we nullify it whenever we think about technique. We cancel out all those hours of practice. This is one of the strongest, most consistent findings in putting science—we putt best when we think about something external to the body, because it brings out our best, automated stroke.

External focus is a powerful strategy to control the putterhead. In one study, researchers asked expert players (handicap five or less) to attempt a series of 10-foot putts, focusing only on trying to hole the putts. They then asked the players to repeat the task, but to say "hit" every time they struck the ball. They holed 20 percent more putts saying hit, compared to not saying hit. Whatever they were thinking about before, saying hit forced the players to focus externally – on the putterhead – and they holed more putts.

This means that our best mental focus during the stroke is something outside the body: the putter, the putterhead, the ball, a part of the ball, an image of the ball rolling towards the hole, or the hole itself. There's even strong evidence that abstract thoughts, such as singing a song, counting backwards from 100 in threes, and thinking about a red Volkswagen all improve skilled performance.

We might prefer, though, to focus on something related to the putt, in which case anything between the hands and the hole allows our brains to deliver our best, automated strokes. And there's evidence that the farther away from our body we direct our thoughts, the better the stroke. In fact, some researchers believe that the brain considers the putter to be part of the body, because we're connected to it, and it's within our 'personal space'. If this is true, focusing on the hole will be more effective. Or the dark side of the moon. Overall, an image of the ball rolling into the hole satisfies the scientific criteria for an ideal external thought.

One important implication of the connection between external focus and automaticity is that we should only change our stroke mechanics in times of desperation. First, changing mechanics – even minimally – takes us many steps backwards in terms of automaticity. We need considerable amounts of practice before the change embeds itself within the motor plan, and automaticity returns. Second, whenever we make a technical change, we tend to monitor it while we're making the stroke, to make sure we're doing it correctly. That is, we focus internally, destroying whatever automaticity remains. This means that tinkering continually with putting technique – something many of us are prone to – is a bad idea. And we should be wary of technical putting tips, however well intentioned!

Pressure and choking

Examples of top players missing short putts when under pressure – choking – abound in golf, and we won't add to anyone's misery by re-living their agonies here. We know that pressure causes choking—but how? There are two theories. The first is that pressure diverts our thoughts. We think about the audience, the victory speech, or the shame of missing, and we don't focus enough on the task in hand. The second theory is that pressure causes the opposite—we focus too hard. We focus internally on technique, trying to be extra careful. The weight of scientific evidence supports the second theory—internal focus is the primary cause of choking. This means we have a cure: we can think about the hole, or a red Volkswagen.

An alternative approach to curing choking is to squeeze the left hand a few times before we putt. It sounds almost too simple, but it works like this. We've already seen how a left-to-right shift in brain activity achieves the optimal mental state for putting. Pressure does the opposite—it reverses the flow. This means that when we're under pressure, we need to take positive steps to ensure our right brain stays in control. The right brain controls the left side of the body, so doing something physical with our left side – like squeezing the left hand – stimulates right-brain activity, keeping us calm.

Researchers in Germany tested this theory by asking soccer players to squeeze a small ball in either their left or right hand before taking a series of penalty kicks under pressure. Three hundred jeering students waiting for a televised soccer match to start (Germany v Austria) applied the pressure. Left-hand squeezers performed equally well under pressure, whereas right-hand squeezers choked badly. The researchers repeated the experiment, using Taekwondo skills and badminton serves, and the results were the same. Left-hand squeezers performed consistently better under pressure. And we don't need a ball—just clenching the left fist has the same effect.

The yips

In extreme cases, choking can manifest itself as the 'yips', a pressure-related affliction similar to 'dartitis' in darts, and 'target fever' in archery. Dartitis prevents darts players from releasing the dart.

Target fever causes archers either to release the arrow prematurely, or to freeze. Golfers with the yips experience muscular jerks, tremors, and freezing in the arms, fingers and hands, which cause erratic strokes, and embarrassing misses.

We can see and measure violent muscular jerks in afflicted golfers, especially in the forearms. The most striking observation is a simultaneous contraction (a 'double pull') of the forearm muscles. Instead of one muscle contracting while its opposite muscle is relaxing, which is the normal pattern, they both contract at the same time—a 'hiccup of the wrist'. Up to 50 percent of golfers have experienced the yips, which in severe cases can cost up to five shots per round.

The yips tend to afflict regular golfers (averaging 75 rounds per year), older and more experienced golfers (more than 25 years playing), and better golfers (single figure handicap). And mostly men. Short putts (2-4 feet) tend to trigger the yips, especially when they're downhill, fast, and have a left to right break (no surprise there …). And they tend to occur during tournament play, when in a winning situation, and on easy but crucial putts. In short, they happen when we're under pressure.

There are two types of yips: *Type 1* (physical causes), and *Type 2* (psychological causes). Most sufferers lie somewhere on a continuum between the two. Type 1 yips is a medical condition, called 'focal dystonia', a neurological condition that causes involuntary muscular contractions. It's a problem in the central nervous system, a deterioration of the motor pathways involved in performing a skill. But focal dystonia afflicts less than 0.1 percent of the population, whereas putting yips afflicts up to 50 percent of golfers, so it's likely that most sufferers have Type 2 yips—a severe case of choking.

For Type 1 yips, there's no real cure. When the body's nervous system is damaged, medical treatment is the only solution. In activities where Type 1 yips are common – for example, writers' and musicians' cramp – many potential cures have been tried, but essentially, there's no simple remedy. Clinical input is required, to assess and treat the condition.

In contrast, Type 2 yips are curable. We've already seen that choking occurs when we allow our attention to wander internally, so our route to curing both choking and the yips is to adopt an external swing thought. Yips sufferers might re-read the previous section on external and internal focus, and experiment with external foci to use when putting under pressure. It's a simple skill, which only takes a second. At the start of the quiet eye period, just before we start the stroke, we need to make sure we focus our attention on something outside the body. Again, an image of the ball falling into the hole is perfect. Annex 2 contains other examples of external foci that can be effective.

PUTTING KEYS

I   An effective putting stroke requires a left-to-right shift in brain activity, before the stroke begins.

I   An external focus of attention stimulates right-brain activity, and allows our automated putting strokes to run off unhindered.

I   An external focus of attention increases the chances of our putting strokes holding up under pressure.

I   Putting yips are usually an extreme form of choking, and can be cured by adopting an external focus of attention.

Part 4

Making it happen

We will not, of course, try any new theories .... We are perfectly content with our present theory of putting, roughly speaking, the 75th theory we have invented this summer.

—Bernard Darwin, 1911

8

Practice

W<small>E KNOW A LOT ABOUT PRACTICE.</small> Physical educators have been teaching fundamental motor skills – running, jumping, throwing, catching, and striking – to children for more than a century, and the same learning principles apply to anyone who plays sport. We all know that practice is important, but we may not know the *type* of practice that's *most* important. Many of us practise putting diligently, but badly.

The key to effective practice is to train all four elements of the skill: vision, imagery, attention, and mechanical control. The chain is only as strong as its weakest link, so it helps if we know what our weakest links are. Training these systems isn't difficult, but it demands more mental application than we're probably used to, so we may find it challenging at first. We'll cover four important areas: deliberate practice, putting without rules, goal setting, and organisation.

Deliberate practice

First, look at Annex 1, which outlines a practice session that addresses all the skill elements. Note that the session is divided into sections, each addressing different elements. Each section also has its own set of learning conditions: whether we use a ball or not, whether we putt to a target or into open space, and whether we use internal or external focus.

The session is a long way removed – in terms of both content and design – from simply putting balls at holes, and seeing how many fall in. It doesn't include endless repetition, which we know is ineffective in developing high-level skill. Mere repetition, while effective in the early stages of putting development, soon leads to performance stagnation—a *learning plateau*. Many of us will have experienced learning plateaus, where no matter what we do in practice, we don't improve. In this situation, we're tempted to try gimmicks, tinker with technique, or change our putter, but this rarely works. The answer lies in changing the way we practise.

Over recent years, we've learnt a lot about a specific, challenging type of practice, designed to improve skills to the highest levels. We call it *deliberate practice,* and it's used by elite performers in many high-skill sports and activities, including musicians, gymnasts, ballet dancers, typists, and golfers.[i] Anders Ericsson, Professor of Psychology at Florida State University, pioneered research in this field. He describes deliberate practice as highly focused, designed to develop all elements of a skill, and aimed at eradicating weaknesses. While many of us will have heard about deliberate practice, or read

---

[i] In the companion book 'The Golf Swing: it's easier than you think', deliberate practice was described in detail, and called *creative practice.*

one of the popular books it has spawned, we shouldn't ignore its importance for high-level skill development, because it's our route to expert putting status.[ii]

Many of us will recognise the typical features of a regular old practice session. We use more than one ball, so we always get second chances; we practise in a non-competitive frame of mind; we don't practise all elements of the skill; we don't putt under pressure; we putt many balls from the same distance. To quote Gary Marcus, Professor of Psychology at New York University: "Most of the practice that most people do, most of the time, be it in the pursuit of learning the guitar or improving their golf game, yields almost no effect".[iii] For most golfers, becoming an expert putter has more to do with *how* we practise than with *how much* we practise. It's quality, not quantity.

Deliberate practice involves reversing all the features of regular old practice, breaking down the skill into its key elements, and devising challenging practice routines to improve each. In particular, it involves improving the *weakest* elements. By practising in this way, we prevent our systems settling for a skill level that 'just about gets the job done'. It's human nature to do this. For example, we've settled for a walking ability that gets us around, but we're not brilliant walkers. We can get food into our mouths comfortably, but we don't hit dead centre every time. And in golf, many of us do the same, settling for the first skill plateau we come across, and staying on the same handicap for years—even decades.

[ii] For example, *The Talent Code*, Daniel Coyle; *Outliers*, Malcolm Gladwell; *Talent is Overrated*, Geoff Colvin; *Bounce*, Mathew Syed.
[iii] In: *Guitar Zero—The New Musician and the Science of Learning.* Penguin Group US, 2012.

We might now read Annex 1 and Annex 2 in more detail, because they contain examples of deliberate practice routines. It isn't a complicated concept. All we need to do is ensure that we stretch our current abilities, by attempting challenging putting tasks that demand effective input from all our control systems.

Putting without rules

It's important not to establish a set of mechanical rules for the putting stroke. The problem with rules is that we're tempted to check if we're sticking to them, by focusing internally on body positions and movements. It's better to dispense with rules, and establish good putting *habits*, which run off automatically, leaving us free to focus on the putt.

Learning a skill without rules means learning it subconsciously, by focusing on *what* we want to happen, not *how* to do it. We focus on the putt, not the stroke. We've known for decades that the human brain, given only an image of the desired result (e.g. the ball falling into the hole), can develop an effective technique to achieve that result without any conscious input from us. The putt drives the mechanics; the mechanics don't drive the putt. This ties in well with the concept of *allowing* our instinctive control systems to guide the stroke, which we discussed in Chapter 6.

We call this *implicit learning.*[iv] We learn all our skills implicitly, and, remarkably, when we've learnt them, we don't know what we've learnt. We don't know, for example, how we tie our shoelaces, sign our names, or button our shirts. We learn these skills without rules, so we never think about how to do them. In putting,

___

[iv] We learn a skill *implicitly* when we learn in the absence of any technical knowledge or advice.

while it's important to establish the mechanical fundamentals discussed in chapter 6, it's even more important not to obsess over the details.

An important consequence of learning without rules is that it prevents choking. We saw in Chapter 7 that the primary cause of choking is our tendency, under pressure, to focus internally. We try extra hard to stick to the movement rules. But when we learn putting implicitly, we can't focus internally, because we don't know what to focus on—we don't know any rules. We can only focus on the putt, and we don't choke. This has important implications for coaching, because by teaching players mechanical rules, we're teaching them to choke.

Of course, most of us have already learnt how to putt, and our minds may be swimming with rules. But we have hope. Even though it's impossible to eradicate the rules, we can overpower them with new, image-based thoughts that divert attention away from mechanics. We never lose old habits and thoughts, but we can replace them. The putting stroke is one of the smallest, simplest movements in sport. The mechanics aren't a problem—controlling them is. Annex 2 contains some 'thought control' practices that will help.

Goal setting

We should set clear goals for putting practice (and for playing …). Goal setting is a huge – and very important – field, and again, it can get complicated, involving a knowledgeable coach and maybe a sport psychologist. But it can also be simple, involving understanding just one key concept: the difference between long-term, 'dream' goals, and short-term, practical goals we can use today.

Our dream putting goal might be to average 30 putts per round over the coming season, or to average no more than one three putt per round. We call these *outcome goals*. The problem with outcome goals is that while they're great to have, they're useless by themselves, because they don't tell us what we need to do today, to take another step towards achieving the goal. We need some short-term goals to use in today's practice or game.

We call short-term goals *process goals*, because they focus on our behaviour—what we need to *do* today. For example, we might have goals such as "I won't three putt today", or "I'll control distance to within 15 percent". These are useful, because we can measure progress against them, but they still don't tell us exactly what to do in order to achieve them. For this, we need the most important type of process goals: goals that relate to how we *think*.

Thinking goals are a mental 'to-do' list for today's efforts. They're critical for effective practice (and play), because they're the only thing under our complete control. Expert putting, as we've seen, is mostly about the way we think, so thinking goals have a major effect on performance. Examples include "I won't replay missed putts over and over in my mind", "I'll take two deep breaths before every pressure putt", "I can't control whether I hole the putt, so I won't get upset when I miss", and "I'll perform my routine consistently for every putt". An important task, after a bad putt, is to avoid asking "What did I *do* wrong?" and instead ask "How did I *think* wrong?"

We should write all our goals down, measure how well we kept to them, and adapt them if they're not working. As we achieve goals, we can set new ones. Goal setting never stops, it's a career-long activity.

Organisation

Most of us are busy, and tend to fit in a bit of putting practice whenever we can. And even those of us who do find more time don't approach sessions with any clear plan. But we should, because how we organise sessions affects how much we improve. Three aspects of organisation are important: putt variety, how often we practise, and whether we putt to a target.

Putt variety refers to whether we attempt the same putt many times, or a different putt each time. We call these methods *blocked* and *random* practice. Random practice produces better results, especially for improving long-putting performance. There are complex reasons for this, but essentially, changing the putt each time disrupts our memory, so we can't use the knowledge gained from a previous putt we hit just a few seconds ago. Every putt is a new challenge, involving all elements of the putting skill—not just a minor adjustment. Expert putters respond particularly well to random practice, whereas novices benefit from blocked practice initially, but should move on to random practice as they improve.

Practice frequency refers to the length and timing of sessions. Multiple, short sessions (called *distributed* practice) yield greater improvement than fewer, longer sessions (called *massed* practice). Shorter sessions prevent fatigue, improve mental focus, and promote permanent retention of what we learn. If we base our practice on the principles of deliberate practice, short sessions are essential, because of the mental effort involved. Long sessions lead to boredom, loss of focus, and mindless repetition. The lounge carpet is an invaluable resource for distributed practice!

Finally, aiming at a hole isn't always a good idea. The problem with aiming at a hole is that we mostly miss, and we wonder why. This leads to an internal focus on mechanics, checking for faults.

We go through a mental process of error–analysis–solution, which can become a frustrating downward spiral, because the more we miss, the more we focus internally, and the more we miss. For these reasons, practice should include some *errorless learning*. As the name suggests, errorless learning is putting without missing, for example, putting from a very short distance. The usual format for errorless learning is to start with a series of short putts that we can't miss, and work gradually further away from the hole. We can't avoid errors, but we can introduce them gradually. An alternative is simply to putt into a vacant area of the green. Annexes 1 and 2 include some examples of errorless learning routines.

We can conclude this section with an acknowledgement that with the best will in the world, many of us have limited practice time, and we devote most of it to attending to our full swing. If we're serious about lowering our scores, we'll find a way to increase our practice time, and devote more of it to putting, but the reality for many of us is that we won't. For those individuals, Annex 3 contains the 'cheat's version'. It distils everything we've covered so far into a 'six-step scientific routine'. It's no substitute for practice, but it may improve things a little!

\/ \/ \/   \/ \/ \/

PUTTING KEYS

- We should divide practice sessions into sections, each with its own set of learning conditions, designed to improve different skill elements.
- Deliberate practice challenges our abilities, addresses our weaknesses, and improves all elements of the skill.
- We learn skills most effectively when we learn them subconsciously.
- Short-term thinking goals are critical to improvement, because they tell us what to do.
- Well-organised practice sessions maximise improvement.

9

Thinking traps

W E HIT BAD PUTTS WITH OUR BRAINS. When we miss a putt, we may believe we made a physical error, but the reality is that we made a mental error—a *thinking* error. The brain controls all our movements, so if we want to control a putt, we need to control our brains. We've already covered some important mental skills, but how we think is such an important aspect of putting that we should consider a few more. We won't delve too deeply into sport psychology, because it's a huge field, and it can get complicated. Instead, we can be selective, and discuss some important psychological skills that are particularly relevant for putting. We'll consider how to avoid some common *thinking traps,* which – should we fall into them – will damage our putting. First, we'll address the *confidence trap*.

The confidence trap

There's nothing wrong with genuine confidence, but there's a lot wrong with false confidence. We're often told that to be good putters we must have confidence, but no one tells us how to get it. The trap here is trying to become instantly confident, rather than earning it through practice.

Most of us have heard of the 'power of positive thinking', which claims that simply believing we can do something gives us the ability to do it. Unfortunately, although a positive attitude is generally good for putting, much of the popular literature surrounding its 'power' is – to put it kindly – exaggerated. In putting, this view has an unhealthy grip, with expert putters saying we must "believe we'll hole every putt". Although well intentioned, this advice ignores the crucial point that expert putters have earned genuine confidence, whereas the rest of us haven't (yet).

The problem with believing we'll hole every putt is that we know we won't. Apart from tap-ins, we know we'll only hole a small handful of putts each round—sometimes we won't hole any! Knowing this, any 'confidence' we have can only be *false* confidence, which triggers a disturbing mental conflict: our minds are awash with 'confident thoughts', but we don't believe them. Under the surface, we're not confident at all, because we have the knowledge of thousands of previous missed putts. We need to earn some genuine confidence, through practice, belief in our stroke, and the knowledge of previous successes.

The nearest we come to believing we can hole every putt is the image we hold of the ball falling into the hole. And it's possible that when expert putters say we must believe we'll hole every putt, they're referring to this imagery, because we know expert putters image in this way. But we shouldn't mistake a healthy image of a ball falling into the hole for believing it will actually happen. The message here is to approach each putt confidently, but to direct that confidence towards our stroke. If we've practised well, and developed a sound mental and physical routine, we *can* have genuine confidence in our ability to make a good stroke.

This has important implications for how we react to misses. When we have false confidence – believing we can hole every putt – misses are disasters. So most putts are disasters. Such regular 'failures' cause negative feelings, which increase hole after hole, until we find ourselves in danger of losing mental control. For every putt, the best we can do is to make our best stroke. We can control that; we can't control whether the ball falls into the hole. In competitive sport, we can only control the controllables, but we can be highly confident in our ability to do that.

When you make a mistake, flush it, and move on.

—Ken Ravizza

The perfectionist's trap

If we're excessively tidy, or iron our socks, we should beware, because it's a sign we may be perfectionists, and it could be harming our putting. Perfectionists set excessively high standards, and are highly critical of themselves when they don't achieve them. Perfectionism can be positive, keeping scientists in the laboratory, pianists at their keyboards, and golfers on the practice green, but unfortunately, it has an unhealthy side.

Problems arise when a player (or parent, or coach) sets goals that are too high for current ability. It's no problem to aim high in the long term – dreaming of being a champion – but aiming too high for today's game or session is a problem, because it creates pressure to achieve the unachievable. We again suffer the mental conflict of needing to achieve something, but knowing we can't.[i] We feel frustrated, guilty, angry, embarrassed, and anxious. For any well-meaning parent or coach, not allowing little Joanna out of the bunker until she's holed a shot isn't the best plan!

Players, parents, and coaches can foster healthy perfectionism by applying only limited pressure to achieve, setting realistic and achievable goals, and adopting a relaxed approach to making mistakes. This isn't a negative approach, it's a proven way of developing a skill by improving both its physical and mental dimensions. Pursuing one without the other is pointless.

Ken Ravizza, Professor of Applied Sports Psychology at California State University, has an excellent strategy for dealing with unhealthy perfectionism. He asks players to walk through a bathtub full of water, and then asks how many managed to walk across the surface without getting their feet wet. Nobody, of course (yet …). He's making the point that only one person is perfect enough to walk on water—the rest of us make mistakes. The ability to deal with failure is a huge part of expert performance.

You need a mental plan for when the garbage hits the fan—because the garbage WILL hit the fan.

—Ken Ravizza

---

[i] The technical term for this conflict of thoughts is *cognitive resonance*. The first use of the term was for members of a UFO cult, who experienced serious mental conflict between their fervent belief in an impending apocalypse, and its failure to arrive.

The talking trap

Many of us talk our way through a putt. "Right, now slowly back, head still, don't peek …." We call this *verbalisation*. Unfortunately, verbalisation is a logical, left-brain activity, which shuts down our right-brain imaging processes—we can either talk about a putt, or picture it, but we can't do both. As we've seen, imaging is crucial to putting, so shutting down this important control system by talking to ourselves can only harm our performance.

Remarkably, verbalising a putt 'offline' also harms performance. Offline verbalisation means thinking, talking, reading, or writing about how we putt. In one study, expert putters took a putting test. Researchers then asked the players to talk for five minutes about how they putt, at the end of which the players retook the test. After the talking session, they holed 50 percent fewer putts. Don't panic, but reading putting books isn't the best plan! In the same way, coaching other people can harm our personal performance, because it always involves offline verbalisation.

When you have to shoot, shoot—don't talk!

—Tuco, in 'The Good, the Bad, and the Ugly'; 1966

The stereotype trap

In the film 'White men can't jump', Billy Hoyle is a former college basketball player who hustles money from California streetballers.[ii] The exclusively black streetballers assume they'll beat him, because he's white. Hoyle always tells the streetballers how good he is, but because of their assumptions about white men – that they're less

---

[ii] 'Streetballers' play street basketball.

athletic – they don't believe him. Hoyle takes all the money. The point is, Hoyle's hustle relies on the blacks' stereotypical view of whites. And such beliefs can damage putting performance, through a process called *stereotype threat*.

Stereotype threat operates when members of a group underperform in a task, because they're trying hard to disprove a general belief that their group lacks ability in that task. Stereotype threat exists in putting, in terms of both race and gender. For example, whites putt worse when told that putting depends on 'athletic ability', because there's a stereotype that whites are athletically inferior to blacks. And blacks putt worse when told that putting depends on 'athletic intelligence', because there's a stereotype that blacks have less. In terms of gender, men putt worse when told that women are better putters, and women putt worse when told that men are better putters.

It's easy to understand the mechanism. When under stereotype threat, individuals *try harder*. Specifically, they focus internally on technique, trying to be extra careful, putt extra well, and disprove the stereotype. But the internal focus destroys their automated stroke, and performance deteriorates. At the time of writing, a well-known golf magazine is carrying a leading article entitled 'Why women putt worse than men'. It's impossible to know how accurate the article is, but it doesn't matter. The important point is that it exists, and women will believe it, strengthening the stereotype threat towards women's putting.

We can employ a number of strategies to overcome negative stereotypes. The key strategy is to recognise that stereotype threat exists, and how it works. Once we understand it – and that it's only a thinking problem – we can ignore it. A second strategy is to know there's no biological reason why either blacks or women should be worse putters. Neither whites nor men possess any special putting talents. We can also overcome stereotype threat by destroying it, through the emergence of elite role models from within the stereotype group. The brilliant putting performances of Tiger Woods and Inbee Park have probably done much to counter both race and gender putting stereotypes.

We may not be there yet, but any of us who are black and/or female can feel comfortable – or at least, less uncomfortable – about our putting abilities.

Feel comfortable feeling uncomfortable—discomfort is what competitive sport is all about.

—Ken Ravizza

The trying trap

We've already mentioned some of the problems of trying hard in the previous section, but we need to know in more detail why it never works. Despite the common belief that trying hard leads to better results, it's best not to try too hard on the putting green.

The problem with trying is that it takes us away from the things we normally do. We move out of our well-practised putting routine, by taking extra time, thinking different thoughts, and looking in different places—things we haven't practised. We practise to develop skills that will stand up to competitive pressure, but if competition forces us outside our skill set, by trying extra hard to hole the putt, we'll be using an inferior and unpractised method.

During competition, we'll hole more putts if we putt as we do in practice. We don't need to 'bring it up a level', because there isn't a level to bring it up to. We can only make our best stroke if we follow our normal, well-practised routine; no extra thought, extra look, or new tactic will improve our stroke just for this putt. Our normal putt is *always* our best putt.

The first step to maintaining our normal routine is to *have* a routine—because many of us don't. The second step is to ensure that it includes the key mental elements of the skill, because we need to *think* the same way each time, not just *do* the same things. Elite performers follow a five-step performance routine, based on figure 17.

Step	Physical	Mental
1. *Prepare*	Position the body	Adopt the mental state in which we give our best performances
2. *Visualise*	–	Create an image of what we're trying to achieve
3. *Focus*	–	Adopt a *single* external thought
4. *Move*	Just do it	Do it with a quiet mind
5. *Evaluate*	–	Compare the result with the plan; Did we follow this routine?

Figure 17. The five-step performance routine.[iii]

Note that the final step, evaluation, takes place after the performance, so it can't affect the quality of the putt. But it might affect the quality of the *next* putt. Note also that the entire routine, after we've positioned our body, is mental. Annex 1 contains practices to develop a putting routine, and Annex 3 is a simple example.

Trying hard never works. When you try hard, you're not trusting yourself.

—Ken Ravizza

[iii] Adapted from reference 136.

The traffic light trap

All the thinking traps we've discussed, if we don't avoid them, lead to negative feelings, which can escalate into something far worse— *losing control*. The cornerstone of sport psychology is that we must first control ourselves, before we can control our performance, so we need to train mentally, just as much as physically. Failure is built into sport, and we need to know what to do when the garbage hits the fan, because, as Ken Ravizza says, it will. We need to know how to stay in control during those 'difficult' moments, when things don't go exactly to plan.

We can consider mental control as a traffic light system:

- **Green** – focused, positive, confident, in control;
- **Amber** – frustrated, distracted, tentative, thoughts starting to spin, losing control;
- **Red** – angry, negative (or apathetic and given up), lost it.

It's important to recognise our personal signs of when we're moving away from the green light, not just for putting, but also for our whole golf game. Behavioural signs include head-shaking, gesticulating, spike mark tapping, putter kicking, and excess self-talk and self-criticism. Physical signs include tense muscles, a faster pulse, sweating, and heightened feelings of annoyance and anger. These are natural reactions to any disappointment, but if we don't catch them early, the move from green to red can be rapid, and we soon find ourselves in a mental zone where we beat ourselves. Some rare sportsmen – John McEnroe and Tiger Woods spring to mind – get frustrated and angry, but they also have skills to deal with it. They flush it, and move on.

Unfortunately, putting is the perfect trigger for losing control, because it involves so much failure. After a missed putt, or a series of missed putts, we become exasperated, and the traffic lights start to change. Sometimes we can get it back, but many times, we can't. We can experience effects on the next tee, where, in a moment of rash decision-making, we go for a long drive, and find ourselves in yet more trouble. In the heat of battle, bad decisions are always emotional decisions, and if we can't control our mental state – our thoughts – bad decisions will escalate.

We need a plan. We need a small armoury of simple mental skills – thinking skills – that we can use to dampen our emotional reactions to missed putts. There are two key strategies. First, before the game, we can take a few moments to remind ourselves how many putts we hole in a good putting round. Usually, it's no more than three or four. If we expect more, we become part of the problem, by setting standards we can't achieve. We leave ourselves open to negative feelings, and leave no room for success—no space for *happy* feelings. Putting becomes a miserable experience, even when performance is good.

Second, we need to allow ourselves to make mistakes—to forgive ourselves. After a missed putt, the proverbial monkey jumps on our back, and reminds us about it constantly, replaying every detail. We need to distract the monkey, by filling our minds with what matters—the next shot. We call this process *segmentation*: dividing the game into small parts, forgetting what's happened, and focusing entirely on the next part.

The key to 'flushing' a missed putt, and moving on, is to adopt a thinking strategy that distracts us from the miss. This isn't easy. We're feeling disappointed and frustrated—even cheated. The skill is to prevent the disappointment from developing into negativity and anger. An important strategy to help us develop thinking skills is to set *thinking goals*, as described in Chapter 8. We can also write down some positive steps we can take to achieve our goals. For example, we can choose some positive thoughts to focus on in moments of stress, which encourage us to leave the past behind, and deal with the next task. We call these *mood words, task-specific words,* or *positive self-statements.* They can be words or phrases.

Mood phrases capture reality: "I made a good stroke"; "bad stuff happens"; "it's only one shot". Task-specific phrases focus on the next shot: "the next shot's just as important"; "get into the next routine"; "failure is the new challenge". Positive self-statements focus on us: "I don't usually do that"; "I'm strong, I can cope"; "I'm good at bouncing back". In the heat of battle, some simple strategies that can help our thinking processes include deep breathing, a smile (even if it's a grimace), and positive body language.

You can't control what happens, but you can control how you choose to respond. You can do everything right and still fail!

—Ken Ravizza

PUTTING KEYS

ǀ We need to earn confidence—we can't just *be* confident.

ǀ Setting excessively high performance goals leads to negative feelings, and slows progress.

ǀ Verbalising a putt destroys our ability to hold a mental image, and harms performance.

ǀ Stereotypical views that some groups are worse at putting harms the performance of individuals in that group.

ǀ Trying hard doesn't work, because it takes us out of our normal routine.

ǀ To stay in control, we need to forget the missed putt, and focus on the next shot.

10

Wrap-up

AS AN ENDNOTE TO THIS BOOK, we should consider one of the most remarkable putting performances of all time. At the 2013 Masters tournament, a 14-year-old boy – an amateur playing in his first professional event – topped the putting statistics. Averaging 27 putts per round, on some of the world's fiercest greens, and without a single three putt in 72 holes, Guan Tianlang out-putted the elite of world golf.

This is remarkable, because it shouldn't happen. A young boy shouldn't be able to nullify the professionals' experience, depth of knowledge, hours of practice, and years of coaching. But he did. We can explain 14-year-olds winning Olympic gold medals in gymnastics and swimming through the advantages of a juvenile body build, but this doesn't apply in putting. Something else is going on.

We should think carefully about Guan's performance, because it may contain the most important putting lesson of all. Children and young people see skill challenges in refreshingly simple terms: ball, hole, ball into hole. Just like food, mouth, food into mouth. This lack of focus on technique allows their innate control systems to guide their movements, allowing them to focus entirely on the putt. Adults, in contrast, tend to overcomplicate things, stifling control systems, freezing limbs and joints, and cluttering brains with technical thoughts. Probably, Guan isn't yet stifled, frozen, or cluttered—he just putts.

There are many examples of players who were good putters in their youth, but became mediocre or poor putters later in their careers, as they exchanged a simple, youthful approach for one of technical complexity. These players try to re-discover their lost skills by adopting ever-more complex techniques and equipment, but it rarely works. Complexity isn't a word the brain understands, so the search for a cure is never-ending. The reality is, these players still have their youthful putting abilities, but they're stifling them. The real solution lies within their own minds.

We'll let Bernard Darwin have the last word:

> *To the person who has never played, putting looks absurdly easy, and in fact, it often is easy to him, until he forgets, as he soon does, how to hit the ball naturally and fearlessly.*

—Bernard Darwin, 1911

\\/ \\/ \\/ ⌐ \\/ \\/ \\/

Annex 1
Deliberate practice session

SECTION 1: CHECKING TECHNIQUE

Skills developed
Technique

Practice conditions
- **Internal focus.** Hands, wrists, feet, shoulders, or whatever.
- **Don't use a ball.** Just check technique, make modifications if necessary, and swing the putter to get used to it. If a ball must be used, putt it into open space and ignore the result.

Key points
- **Focus only on the body.** Parts, positions, and movements.
- **Focus on feel.** Sense the technique.
- **Repeat.** Do it enough times to achieve a degree of automaticity. There's no magic number. More is better.

Notes
The point of this preliminary section is to deal with anything that requires internal focus, before we move on to external-focus activities. It should be a short section.

SECTION 2: STROKE MECHANICS

Skills developed

Putterhead path and tempo.

Practice conditions

- *I* **Forget section 1.** No internal focus from this point onwards.
- *I* **External focus.** The putterhead is best.
- *I* **Use a ball.** But don't putt at a hole. Putt into vacant spaces on the green, and ignore the result.
- *I* **Use an aiming line.** Putt the ball so the line doesn't wobble.

Key points

- *I* **Individual build** determines the natural putterhead path and face angle change.
- *I* **Double tempo stroke:** slower, shorter backswing; faster, driven downswing; longer follow-through.
- *I* **Count the putt,** to an even 1–2–3 tempo (not seconds, slightly faster). 2 is the end of the backswing, 3 is impact. Or tick-tick-tock.
- *I* **Vary the putt distance**, but keep the same 1–2–3 tempo.
- *I* **Loosen up** the rigid pendulum.

Notes

It's important not to putt at a target, so we isolate the movement skill. We mustn't yet concern ourselves with judgement, visualisation, gaze patterns, etc. We also avoid the problems of over-analysing misses.

SECTION 3: VISION

Skills developed
Visualisation, gaze pattern, imagery, quiet eye period.

Practice conditions
- **Forget sections 1 and 2**. Stroke mechanics must now take care of themselves.
- **Use a target**. The hole.
- **Vary the putt**. Change distance and slope complexity.
- **External focus**. The hole, or the ball falling into the hole.

Key points
- **Visualise** the perfect putt.
- **Consistent routine:**

  2–3 longer gazes at the hole, 3–4 seconds each;

  Shorter gazes at the ball in between;

  Fast gaze transitions between the two;

  Final gaze at the ball, 1–1.5 seconds;

  Short-to-long, double-tempo stroke;

  Hold gaze steady for a moment after impact.
- **Use the full routine** for every putt.

Notes
A natural progression is to develop the stroke to a 1–5 count, starting when the gaze returns to the ball for the final time. 1–2 is the final gaze at the ball; 3–4 is the backswing; 5 is impact. Again, the count isn't in seconds, it's faster. This routine incorporates both the quiet eye period and the double-tempo stroke.

Annex 2
Practice routines

THIS ANNEX CONTAINS SIMPLE, but challenging routines that can be included in sessions as required. They will help develop our motor control systems, and improve specific elements of the putting skill.

Putting billiards

Place two balls one foot apart. Putt one ball so that it hits the second ball, moving it forward. Repeat until you miss, or can no longer move the second ball in a forward direction. How far can you move the second ball? Across the green is excellent. What's the fewest number of strokes you can take to get across the green?

Thought control

Judge a putt, take your stance, and prepare to make the stroke. Just before you start the backswing, do one of the following, and continue until after impact:

> Think of a red Volkswagen;
>
> Sing a song;
>
> Count backwards from 100;
>
> Recite a mantra that fits a double-tempo stroke, e.g. 'tick–tick–tock';
>
> Say 'hit' as the putterhead strikes the ball;
>
> Think of a person of your choice.

Experiment.

Par putting

Write the numbers 1, 2, 3, 4, 5, 6, 7, 8, 9, and 10 on pieces of paper, and put them in your pocket. Pull out one piece of paper, and pace out that number of paces from the hole. Make a putt from that distance, giving it maximum attention. Repeat for the remaining pieces of paper. Hole out any second putt that isn't an obvious 'gimme' (don't cheat). Keep score (par = 20). Only do this once per session—putting doesn't give second chances.

Visit the Himalayas

This will need a trip to St. Andrews, but if you do happen to be in the vicinity, visit the Himalayas, also known as the 'Ladies Putting Green'.[i] It's a long, mountainous putting green, where holes in one are rare. The 'clubhouse' is adjacent to the first tees of the New and Jubilee courses. The course record is a remarkable 34. It's perfect, because it's *challenging.*

These are just a few examples of practices that challenge our control systems, and force them to adapt and improve. We can create our own, as long as we remember to target specific elements of the skill, especially the weaker elements.

---

[i] Home page: http://nell111.webs.com/

Annex 3
The six-step putting routine

SOME OF US ARE IMPATIENT. We just want some simple advice on how to improve our putting stroke next Saturday—earlier, if possible. We need the 'putting in a nutshell' version, so here's a simple, six-step approach to a scientific putting routine. It's no substitute for practice, but it's worth a try.

1. Judge speed and line;
2. Imagine the putt;
3. Take a long look at the hole;
4. Take a short look at the ball and think about the hole;
5. Make a short-to-long stroke;
6. Smile.

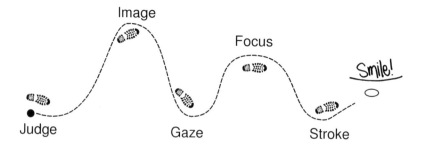

Annex 4
Bibliography

THE REFERENCE LIST BELOW contains selected scientific articles used in writing this book. Abstracts of most articles can be downloaded free of charge from academic databases, such as *Pub Med*: http://www.ncbi.nlm.nih.gov/pubmed/. Full-length articles can sometimes be downloaded free of charge, but most require a journal subscription or purchase. Free abstracts, and a larger selection of full-length articles can be obtained from *Google Scholar*: http://scholar.google.com/. Copyright restrictions prevent the author from supplying copies of articles.

Judging speed and line

1. Bowen, R. T. Putting errors of beginning golfers using different points of aim. *Research quarterly* **39**, 31–5 (1968).

2. Grober, R. The geometry of putting on a planar surface. *Journal of Applied Golf Research* (2011).

3. Hoadley, B. How to lower your putting score without improving. *Science and golf II: Proceedings from the world scientific congress of golf* 186–192 (1994).

4. Holmes, B. Putting: how golf ball and hole interact. *American Journal of Physics* **59**, 129–136 (1990).

5. Koslow, R. & Wenos, D. Realistic expectations on the putting green: within and between days trueness of roll. *Perceptual and motor skills* **87**, 1441–2 (1998).

6. MacKenzie, S. J. & Sprigings, E. J. Evaluation of the plumb-bob method for reading greens in putting. *Journal of sports sciences* **23**, 81–7 (2005).

7. Naito, K., Kato, T. & Fukuda, T. Expertise and position of line of

sight in golf putting. *Perceptual and motor skills* **99**, 163–70 (2004).

8. Pelz, D. *Putt like the pros*. (Harper Perennial: New York, 1989).

9. Penner, R. The physics of putting. *Canadian journal of physics* **80**, 1–14 (2002).

10. Penner, R. The physics of golf. *Reports on progress in physics* **66**, 131–171 (2003).

11. Templeton, H. *Vector putting*. (Vector Golf inc.: 1984).

12. Vanderbei, R. A case study in trajectory optimisation: putting on an uneven green. *SIAG/OPT Views-and-News* **12**, 6–14 (2001).

13. Vanderbei, R. Case studies in trajectory optimisation: trains, planes and other pastimes. *Optimisation and engineering* **2**, 215–243 (2001).

Vision, perception, and imagery

14. Aksamit, G. & Husak, W. Feedback influences on the skill of putting. *Perceptual and motor skills* **56**, 19–22 (1983).

15. Badami, R., VaezMousavi, M., Wulf, G. & Namazizadeh, M. Feedback about more accurate versus less accurate trials: differential effects on self-confidence and activation. *Research quarterly for exercise and sport* **83**, 196–203 (2012).

16. Bansal, M. & Broadie, M. A simulation model to analyze the impact of hole size on putting in golf. *Simulation conference, 2008. Winter* 2826–2834 (2008).

17. Baumeister, J., Reinecke, K., Cordes, M., Lerch, C. & Weiss, M. Brain activity in goal-directed movements in a real compared to a virtual environment using the Nintendo Wii. *Neuroscience letters* **481**, 47–50 (2010).

18. Baumeister, J., Reinecke, K., Liesen, H. & Weiss, M. Cortical activity of skilled performance in a complex sports related motor task. *European journal of applied physiology* **104**, 625–31 (2008).

19. Behan, M. & Wilson, M. State anxiety and visual attention: the role of the quiet eye period in aiming to a far target. *Journal of sports sciences* **26**, 207–15 (2008).

20. Beilock, S. L., Bertenthal, B. I., Hoerger, M. & Carr, T. H. When does

haste make waste? Speed-accuracy trade-off, skill level, and the tools of the trade. *Journal of experimental psychology. Applied* **14**, 340–52 (2008).

21. Beilock, S. L. & Gonso, S. Putting in the mind versus putting on the green: expertise, performance time, and the linking of imagery and action. *Quarterly journal of experimental psychology (2006)* **61**, 920–32 (2008).

22. Beilock, S. L., Wierenga, S. A. & Carr, T. H. Expertise, attention, and memory in sensorimotor skill execution: impact of novel task constraints on dual-task performance and episodic memory. *The Quarterly journal of experimental psychology. A, Human experimental psychology* **55**, 1211–40 (2002).

23. Bulson, R. C., Ciuffreda, K. J. & Hung, G. K. The effect of retinal defocus on golf putting. *Ophthalmic & physiological optics : the journal of the British College of Ophthalmic Opticians (Optometrists)* **28**, 334–44 (2008).

24. Cañal-Bruland, R., Pijpers, J. R. & Oudejans, R. R. D. Close, and a cigar!--Why size perception relates to performance. *Perception* **41**, 354–6 (2012).

25. Cañal-Bruland, R., Zhu, F. F., der Kamp, J. van & Masters, R. S. W. Target-directed visual attention is a prerequisite for action-specific perception. *Acta psychologica* **136**, 285–9 (2011).

26. Causer, J., Bennett, S. J., Holmes, P. S., Janelle, C. M. & Williams, A. M. Quiet eye duration and gun motion in elite shotgun shooting. *Medicine and science in sports and exercise* **42**, 1599–608 (2010).

27. Causer, J., Holmes, P. S. & Williams, A. M. Quiet eye training in a visuomotor control task. *Medicine and science in sports and exercise* **43**, 1042–9 (2011).

28. Clark, J. F., Ellis, J. K., Bench, J., Khoury, J. & Graman, P. High-performance vision training improves batting statistics for University of Cincinnati baseball players. *PloS one* **7**, e29109 (2012).

29. Cockerill, I. M. Visual control in putting. *Psychology of motor behaviour and sport* 377–384 (1979).

117

30. Coelho, C. J., Nusbaum, H. C., Rosenbaum, D. A. & Fenn, K. M. Imagined actions aren't just weak actions: task variability promotes skill learning in physical practice but not in mental practice. *Journal of experimental psychology. Learning, memory, and cognition* **38**, 1759–64 (2012).

31. Derakshan, N., Ansari, T. L., Hansard, M., Shoker, L. & Eysenck, M. W. Anxiety, inhibition, efficiency, and effectiveness. An investigation using antisaccade task. *Experimental psychology* **56**, 48–55 (2009).

32. Di Rienzo, F., Collet, C., Hoyek, N. & Guillot, A. Selective effect of physical fatigue on motor imagery accuracy. *PloS one* **7**, e47207 (2012).

33. Gonzalez, D. A., Kegel, S., Ishikura, T. & Lee, T. Effects of vision on head-putter coordination in golf. *Motor control* **16**, 371–85 (2012).

34. Horn, R. R., Okumura, M. S., Alexander, M. G. F., Gardin, F. A. & Sylvester, C. T. Quiet eye duration is responsive to variability of practice and to the axis of target changes. *Research quarterly for exercise and sport* **83**, 204–11 (2012).

35. Kasper, R. W., Elliott, J. C. & Giesbrecht, B. Multiple measures of visual attention predict novice motor skill performance when attention is focused externally. *Human movement science* **31**, 1161–74 (2012).

36. Kim, S. Gaze behaviour of elite soccer goalkeepers in successful penalty kick defence. *International journal of applied sports sciences* **18**, 96–110 (2006).

37. Lee, C., Linkenauger, S. A., Bakdash, J. Z., Joy-Gaba, J. A. & Profitt, D. R. Putting like a pro: the role of positive contagion in golf performance and perception. *PloS one* **6**, e26016 (2011).

38. Lier, W. van, Kamp, J. & Savelsbergh, G. Gaze in putting: effects of slope. *International journal of sport psychology* **41**, 160–176 (2010).

39. Loze, G. M., Collins, D. & Holmes, P. S. Pre-shot EEG alpha-power reactivity during expert air-pistol shooting: a comparison of best and worst shots. *Journal of sports sciences* **19**, 727–33 (2001).

40. Mackenzie, S. J., Foley, S. M. & Adamczyk, A. P. Visually focusing

on the far versus the near target during the putting stroke. *Journal of sports sciences* **29**, 1243–51 (2011).

41. Mann, D. T. Y., Williams, A. M., Ward, P. & Janelle, C. M. Perceptual-cognitive expertise in sport: a meta-analysis. *Journal of sport & exercise psychology* **29**, 457–78 (2007).

42. Moore, L. J., Vine, S. J., Cooke, A., Ring, C. & Wilson, M. R. Quiet eye training expedites motor learning and aids performance under heightened anxiety: the roles of response programming and external attention. *Psychophysiology* **49**, 1005–15 (2012).

43. Piras, A. & Vickers, J. N. The effect of fixation transitions on quiet eye duration and performance in the soccer penalty kick: instep versus inside kicks. *Cognitive processing* **12**, 245–55 (2011).

44. Proffitt, D. R., Creem, S. H. & Zosh, W. D. Seeing mountains in molehills: geographical-slant perception. *Psychological science* **12**, 418–23 (2001).

45. Roberts, R., Callow, N., Hardy, L., Woodman, T. & Thomas, L. Interactive effects of different visual imagery perspectives and narcissism on motor performance. *Journal of sport & exercise psychology* **32**, 499–517 (2010).

46. Roberts, R. & Turnbull, O. H. Putts that get missed on the right: investigating lateralized attentional biases and the nature of putting errors in golf. *Journal of sports sciences* **28**, 369–74 (2010).

47. Steinberg, G. M., Frehlich, S. G. & Tennant, L. K. Dextrality and eye position in putting performance. *Perceptual and motor skills* **80**, 635–40 (1995).

48. Taylor, J. A. & Shaw, D. F. The effects of outcome imagery on golf-putting performance. *Journal of sports sciences* **20**, 607–13 (2002).

49. Taylor, J. E. T., Witt, J. K. & Sugovic, M. When walls are no longer barriers: perception of wall height in parkour. *Perception* **40**, 757–60 (2011).

50. van Lier, W. H., van der Kamp, J. & Savelsbergh G, J. P. Perception and action in golf putting: skill differences reflect calibration. *Journal of sport & exercise psychology* **33**, 349–69 (2011).

51. Van Lier, W., Van der Kamp, J., van der Zanden, A. & Savelsbergh, G. J. P. No transfer of calibration between action and perception in learning a golf putting task. *Attention, perception & psychophysics* **73**, 2298–308 (2011).

52. Vickers, J. N. Gaze control in putting. *Perception* **21**, 117–32 (1992).

53. Vickers, J. N. Mind over muscle: the role of gaze control, spatial cognition, and the quiet eye in motor expertise. *Cognitive processing* **12**, 219–22 (2011).

54. Vickers, J. N. Advances in coupling perception and action: the quiet eye as a bidirectional link between gaze, attention, and action. *Progress in brain research* **174**, 279–88 (2009).

55. Vickers, J. N. Neuroscience of the quiet eye during golf putting. *International journal of golf science* **1**, 2–9 (2012).

56. Vine, S. J., Moore, L. J. & Wilson, M. R. Quiet eye training facilitates competitive putting performance in elite golfers. *Frontiers in psychology* **2**, 8 (2011).

57. Vine, S. J. & Wilson, M. R. The influence of quiet eye training and pressure on attention and visuo-motor control. *Acta psychologica* **136**, 340–6 (2011).

58. Williams, A. M., Singer, R. N. & Frehlich, S. G. Quiet eye duration, expertise, and task complexity in near and far aiming tasks. *Journal of motor behavior* **34**, 197–207 (2002).

59. Wilson, M. R., Miles, C. A. L., Vine, S. J. & Vickers, J. N. Quiet eye distinguishes children of high and low motor coordination abilities. *Medicine and science in sports and exercise* (2012).

60. Wilson, M. R. & Pearcy, R. C. Visuomotor control of straight and breaking golf putts. *Perceptual and motor skills* **109**, 555–62 (2009).

61. Wilson, M. R. *et al.* Gaze training enhances laparoscopic technical skill acquisition and multi-tasking performance: a randomized, controlled study. *Surgical endoscopy* **25**, 3731–9 (2011).

62. Witt, J. K. & Dorsch, T. E. Kicking to bigger uprights: field goal kicking performance influences perceived size. *Perception* **38**, 1328–40 (2009).

63. Witt, J. K., Linkenauger, S. A., Bakdash, J. Z. & Proffitt, D. R. Putting to a bigger hole: golf performance relates to perceived size. *Psychonomic bulletin & review* **15**, 581–5 (2008).

64. Witt, J. K., Linkenauger, S. A. & Proffitt, D. R. Get me out of this slump! Visual illusions improve sports performance. *Psychological science* **23**, 397–9 (2012).

65. Witt, J. K. & Proffitt, D. R. Action-specific influences on distance perception: a role for motor simulation. *Journal of experimental psychology. Human perception and performance* **34**, 1479–92 (2008).

66. Witt, J. K., Schuck, D. M. & Taylor, J. E. T. Action-specific effects underwater. *Perception* **40**, 530–7 (2011).

67. Witt, J. K. & Sugovic, M. Performance and ease influence perceived speed. *Perception* **39**, 1341–53 (2010).

68. Wood, G. & Wilson, M. R. A moving goalkeeper distracts penalty takers and impairs shooting accuracy. *Journal of sports sciences* **28**, 937–46 (2010).

69. Wood, G. & Wilson, M. R. Quiet-eye training for soccer penalty kicks. *Cognitive processing* **12**, 257–66 (2011).

70. Woolfolk, R., Parrish, M. & Murphy, S. The effect of positive and negative imagery on motor skill and performance. *Cognitive therapy and research* **9**, 335–341 (1985).

Stroke mechanics

71. Chapman, A. How errors in net joint torques affect putter head motion in different putting techniques: a simulation study. *Journal of Applied Golf Research* (2012).

72. Chen, J., Yang, C., Chan, C. & Tang, W. The correlation of golf putting club head velocity and grip force for each phase. *ISBS-conference proceedings archive* **1**, (2008).

73. Chiero, J. Golf putting and postural stability: stance width influences on static postural stability and putter kinematics. PhD thesis (2012).

74. Craig, C. M., Delay, D., Grealy, M. A., & Lee, D. N. Guiding the

swing in golf putting. *Nature* **405**, 295–6 (2000).

75. De Gunther, R. *The art and science of putting.* (Masters Press: Chicago, 1996).

76. Delphinus, E. M. & Sayers, M. G. L. Putting proficiency: contributions of the pelvis and trunk. *Sports biomechanics / International Society of Biomechanics in Sports* **11**, 212–22 (2012).

77. Gott, E. A. & McGown, C. The effects of a combination of stances and points of aim on putting accuracy. *Perceptual and motor skills* **66**, 139–143 (1988).

78. Grober, R. Resonance as a means of distance control in putting. *Open access article; arxiv 1103.2827* (2011).

79. Grober, R. Resonance in putting. *Open access article; arxiv 0903.1762* (2011)

80. Hung, G. K. Effect of putting grip on eye and head movements during the golf putting stroke. *TheScientificWorldJournal* **3**, 122–37 (2003).

81. Karlsen, J. Performance in golf putting. PhD thesis (2010).

82. Karlsen, J. & Nilsson, J. Distance variability ain golf putting among highly skilled players: the role of green reading. *International journal of sports science and coaching* **3**, 71–80 (2008).

83. Karlsen, J., Smith, G. & Nilsson, J. The stroke has only a minor influence on direction consistency in golf putting among elite players. *Journal of sports sciences* **26**, 243–50 (2008).

84. Keogh, J. W. L. & Hume, P. A. Evidence for biomechanics and motor learning research improving golf performance. *Sports biomechanics / International Society of Biomechanics in Sports* **11**, 288–309 (2012).

85. Lee, T. D., Ishikura, T., Kegel, S., Gonzalez, D. & Passmore, S. Head-putter coordination patterns in expert and less skilled golfers. *Journal of motor behavior* **40**, 267–72 (2008).

86. Mackenzie, S. J. & Evans, D. B. Validity and reliability of a new method for measuring putting stroke kinematics using the TOMI system. *Journal of sports sciences* **28**, 891–9 (2010).

87. McLaughlin, P. & Best, R. Taxonomy of golf putting: Do different

golf putting techniques exist? *Journal of sports sciences* **31**, 1038–44 (2013).

88. Neumann, D. L. & Thomas, P. R. The relationship between skill level and patterns in cardiac and respiratory activity during golf putting. *International journal of psychophysiology : official journal of the International Organization of Psychophysiology* **72**, 276–82 (2009).

89. Panchuk, D. & Vickers, J. N. Effect of narrowing the base of support on the gait, gaze, and quiet eye of elite ballet dancers and controls. *Cognitive processing* **12**, 267–76 (2011).

90. Richardson, A., Hughes, G. & Mitchell, A. Centre of pressure excursion during the golf putting stroke in low, mid, and high handicap golfers. *International journal of golf science* (2012).

91. Sim, M. & Kim, J.-U. Differences between experts and novices in kinematics and accuracy of golf putting. *Human movement science* **29**, 932–46 (2010).

92. Tierney, D. & Coop, R. A bivariate probability model for putting proficiency. *Science and golf III: Proceedings of the world scientific congress on golf* 385–394 (1998).

Controlling the stroke

93. Adler, C. H. *et al.* Are the yips a task-specific dystonia or "golfer's cramp"? *Movement disorders : official journal of the Movement Disorder Society* **26**, 1993–6 (2011).

94. Babiloni, C. *et al.* Golf putt outcomes are predicted by sensorimotor cerebral EEG rhythms. *The Journal of physiology* **586**, 131–9 (2008).

95. Bawden, M. & Maynard, I. Towards an understanding of the personal experience of the "yips" in cricketers. *Journal of sports sciences* **19**, 937–53 (2001).

96. Beckmann, J., Gröpel, P. & Ehrlenspiel, F. Preventing motor skill failure through hemisphere-specific priming: cases from choking under pressure. *Journal of experimental psychology. General* (2012).

97. Beilock, S. L. & Gray, R. From attentional control to attentional spill-

over: a skill-level investigation of attention, movement, and performance outcomes. *Human movement science* **31**, 1473–99 (2012).

98. Binsch, O., Oudejans, R. R. D., Bakker, F. C. & Savelsbergh, G. J. P.
Ironic effects and final target fixation in a penalty-shooting task. *Human movement science* **29**, 277–88 (2010).

99. Bright, J. E. & Freedman, O. Differences between implicit and ex-
plicit acquisition of a complex motor skill under pressure: an examination of some evidence. *British journal of psychology* **89 (Pt 2)**, 249–
63 (1998).

100. Cooke, A., Kavussanu, M., McIntyre, D., Boardley, I. D. & Ring, C.
Effects of competitive pressure on expert performance: underlying
psychological, physiological, and kinematic mechanisms. *Psychophysiology* **48**, 1146–56 (2011).

101. Cooke, A., Kavussanu, M., McIntyre, D. & Ring, C. Psychological,
muscular and kinematic factors mediate performance under pressure. *Psychophysiology* **47**, 1109–18 (2010).

102. Crews, D. J. & Landers, D. M. Electroencephalographic measures of
attentional patterns prior to the golf putt. *Medicine and science in
sports and exercise* **25**, 116–26 (1993).

103. de la Peña, D., Murray, N. P. & Janelle, C. M. Implicit overcompen-
sation: the influence of negative self-instructions on performance of
a self-paced motor task. *Journal of sports sciences* **26**, 1323–31 (2008).

104. Delay, D., Nougier, V., Orliaguet, J.-P. & Coello, Y. Movement control in golf putting. *Human movement science* 597–619 (1997).

105. Ehrlenspiel, F., Wei, K. & Sternad, D. Open-loop, closed-loop and
compensatory control: performance improvement under pressure in
a rhythmic task. *Experimental brain research.* **201**, 729–41 (2010).

106. Flegal, K. E. & Anderson, M. C. Overthinking skilled motor performance: or why those who teach can't do. *Psychonomic bulletin & review* **15**, 927–32 (2008).

107. Gray, R. & Beilock, S. L. Hitting is contagious: experience and action
induction. *Journal of experimental psychology. Applied* **17**, 49–59 (2011).

108. Hill, L. Mental representation mediation in expert golf putting. PhD

thesis (2007).

109. Hommel, B. *et al.* How the brain blinks: towards a neurocognitive model of the attentional blink. *Psychological research* **70**, 425–35 (2006).

110. Lam, W. K., Maxwell, J. P. & Masters, R. S. W. Probing the allocation of attention in implicit (motor) learning. *Journal of sports sciences* **28**, 1543–54 (2010).

111. Lam, W. K., Masters, R. S. W. & Maxwell, J. P. Cognitive demands of error processing associated with preparation and execution of a motor skill. *Consciousness and cognition* **19**, 1058–61 (2010).

112. Land, W. & Tenenbaum, G. An outcome and process oriented examination of a golf specific secondary task strategy to prevent choking under pressure. *Journal of applied sport psychology* **24**, 303–322 (2012).

113. Lawrence, G. P., Gottwald, V. M., Khan, M. A. & Kramer, R. S. S. The Movement Kinematics and Learning Strategies Associated with Adopting Different Foci of Attention during Both Acquisition and Anxious Performance. *Frontiers in psychology* **3**, 468 (2012).

114. Maxwell, J. P., Masters, R. S. & Eves, F. F. From novice to no know-how: a longitudinal study of implicit motor learning. *Journal of sports sciences* **18**, 111–20 (2000).

115. Maxwell, J. P., Masters, R. S., Kerr, E. & Weedon, E. The implicit benefit of learning without errors. *The Quarterly journal of experimental psychology. A, Human experimental psychology* **54**, 1049–68 (2001).

116. Mezaki, T. Dystonia as a common status against a common belief. *Clinical neurology* **52**, 1068–70 (2012).

117. Moore, L. J., Vine, S. J., Wilson, M. R. & Freeman, P. The effect of challenge and threat states on performance: an examination of potential mechanisms. *Psychophysiology* **49**, 1417–25 (2012).

118. Oliveira, F. T. P. & Goodman, D. Conscious and effortful or effortless and automatic: a practice/performance paradox in motor learning. *Perceptual and motor skills* **99**, 315–24 (2004).

119. Peh, S. Y.-C., Chow, J. Y. & Davids, K. Focus of attention and its impact on movement behaviour. *Journal of science and medicine in sport / Sports Medicine Australia* **14**, 70–8 (2011).

120. Perkins-Ceccato, N., Passmore, S. R. & Lee, T. D. Effects of focus of attention depend on golfers' skill. *Journal of sports sciences* **21**, 593–600 (2003).

121. Poolton, J. M., Masters, R. S. W. & Maxwell, J. P. The relationship between initial errorless learning conditions and subsequent performance. *Human movement science* **24**, 362–78 (2005).

122. Schorer, J., Jaitner, T., Wollny, R., Fath, F. & Baker, J. Influence of varying focus of attention conditions on dart throwing performance in experts and novices. *Experimental brain research. Experimentelle Hirnforschung. Expérimentation cérébrale* **217**, 287–97 (2012).

123. Shafizadeh, M., McMorris, T. & Sproule, J. Effect of different external attention of focus instruction on learning of golf putting skill. *Perceptual and motor skills* **113**, 662–70 (2011).

124. Smith, A. M. *et al.* A multidisciplinary study of the "yips" phenomenon in golf: An exploratory analysis. *Sports medicine (Auckland, N.Z.)* **30**, 423–37 (2000).

125. Smith, A. M. *et al.* The "yips" in golf: a continuum between a focal dystonia and choking. *Sports medicine (Auckland, N.Z.)* **33**, 13–31 (2003).

126. Southard, D. & Amos, B. Rhythmicity and pre-performance ritual: stabilizing a flexible system. *Research quarterly for exercise and sport* **67**, 288–96 (1996).

127. Stinear, C. M. *et al.* The yips in golf: multimodal evidence for two subtypes. *Medicine and science in sports and exercise* **38**, 1980–9 (2006).

128. Tanaka, Y. & Sekiya, H. The influence of audience and monetary reward on the putting kinematics of expert and novice golfers. *Research quarterly for exercise and sport* **81**, 416–24 (2010).

129. Toner, J. & Moran, A. The effects of conscious processing on golf putting proficiency and kinematics. *Journal of sports sciences* **29**, 673–83 (2011).

130. Zhu, F. F., Poolton, J. M., Wilson, M. R., Maxwell, J. P. & Masters, R. S. W. Neural co-activation as a yardstick of implicit motor learning and the propensity for conscious control of movement. *Biological psychology* **87**, 66–73 (2011).

Making it happen

131. Beilock, S. L., Jellison, W. A., Rydell, R. J., McConnell, A. R. & Carr, T. H. On the causal mechanisms of stereotype threat: can skills that don't rely heavily on working memory still be threatened? *Personality & social psychology bulletin* **32**, 1059–71 (2006).

132. Ericsson, K. & Charness, N. Expert performance. *American psychologist* **49**, 725–747 (1994).

133. Keogh, J. & Hume, P. Practice conditions: how do they influence motor learning in golf? *30th annual conference of biomechanics in sports. Melbourne 2012* 367–370 (2012).

134. Macphail, W. Performance under pressure: the effect of explanatory style on sensory-motor performance under stereotype threat. PhD thesis (2011).

135. van de Pol P, K. C., Kavussanu, M. & Ring, C. The effects of training and competition on achievement goals, motivational responses, and performance in a golf-putting task. *Journal of sport & exercise psychology* **34**, 787–807 (2012).

136. Singer, RN. Strategies and metastrategies in learning and performing self-paced athletic skills. *Sport Psychologist* **2**, 49-68 (1988).

137. Walker, M. P., Brakefield, T., Morgan, A., Hobson, J. A. & Stickgold, R. Practice with sleep makes perfect: sleep-dependent motor skill learning. *Neuron* **35**, 205–11 (2002).

138. Wegner, D., Ansfield, M. & Pilloff, D. The putt and the pendulum: ironic effects of the mental control of action. *Psychological science* **9**, 196–199 (1998).

139. Wulf, G. Attentional focus effects in balance acrobats. *Research quarterly for exercise and sport* **79**, 319–25 (2008).

140. Wulf, G., Shea, C. & Lewthwaite, R. Motor skill learning and performance: a review of influential factors. *Medical education* **44**, 75–84 (2010).

Index

Made in the USA
Columbia, SC
24 April 2017